Diversity in Faith–
Unity in Christ

Diversity in Faith–
Unity in Christ

Shirley C. Guthrie, Jr.

The Westminster Press
Philadelphia

Scripture quotations are from the Revised Standard Version of the Bible, copyrighted 1946, 1952, © 1971, 1973 by the Division of Christian Education of the National Council of the Churches of Christ in the U.S.A., and are used by permission.

Book design by Pat Steiner

First edition

Published by The Westminster Press®
Philadelphia, Pennsylvania

PRINTED IN THE UNITED STATES OF AMERICA
2 4 6 8 9 7 5 3 1

Library of Congress Cataloging-in-Publication Data

Guthrie, Shirley C., 1927–
    Diversity in faith—unity in Christ.

    Bibliography: p.
    Includes index.
    1. Christian life—Presbyterian authors. I. Title.
BV4501.2.G865 1986 248.4′851 86-9157
ISBN 0-664-24013-5 (pbk.)

For Vivian and Tom

Contents

Foreword

The Thomas White Currie Lectures given by Professor Shirley Guthrie at Austin Presbyterian Theological Seminary in February 1985 form the core of this volume. Professor Guthrie, in both his original presentations and in this book, ably fulfills the intent of the Highland Park Presbyterian Church's Tom Currie Bible Class; namely, to honor the late Dr. Thomas White Currie, president of the Seminary from 1922 to 1943, and Interim Pastor and teacher of the Currie Class of Highland Park Presbyterian Church from 1932 to 1937.

Professor Guthrie's discussion of contemporary theology and its significance for the church's life contributes to the ongoing discussion about how faith in Jesus Christ is and might be understood in the contemporary world. He illustrates the importance of what President Currie struggled in both church and seminary to ensure, that faith and thinking would be partners in the service of God's kingdom. This volume is a distinguished addition to the literature stimulated by the Currie Lectureship.

JACK L. STOTTS, *President*
Austin Presbyterian Theological Seminary
Austin, Texas

Preface
and Acknowledgments

The task of Christian theology is the church's task, not that of lone individuals. This is a quite different book from what it would have been without the contribution of fellow Christians and Christian communities.

I shared earlier versions of these pages with many groups of lay people and ministers. They raised questions and made constructive suggestions that led to many changes as I prepared this final version. I hope those who read it will recognize how much I learned from them.

My conversations with these groups might never have become a book if I had not been invited to deliver the Thomas White Currie Lectures at Austin Presbyterian Theological Seminary in the winter of 1985. The helpful criticisms of faculty, students, alumnae, and alumni led to further revisions of the material, and their friendly response encouraged me to put it into book form.

My colleagues C. Benton Kline, Charles B. Cousar, and George W. Stroup taught me as I worked and helped me to clarify and correct what I wrote. With other faculty members and students at Columbia Theological Seminary, and with my wife, Vivian, and son, Tom, they also helped by taking seriously but not too seriously my constant complaints about the difficulty of writing and finding time to write.

I never forget that I would not be teaching and writing theology today if Roseanneli and Donald Leverett had not made graduate study possible for me when I finished my seminary education. And I remain grateful to the members of the First Presbyterian Church of Rusk, Texas, who helped a young theologian become a pastor and who have been my friends through the years.

Ann Titshaw, mother of us all on the third floor where I work, typed the manuscript and encouraged me to hope that it was worth typing.

SHIRLEY C. GUTHRIE, JR.

Introduction

This is a book about what it means to be a Christian. I will be pleased if some non-Christians read it to find out what Christian faith and life are all about, but it is addressed primarily to other Christians. Its purpose is not so much to help non-Christians learn what it means to be a Christian as to help us Christians learn.

At first glance it may seem unnecessary and even insulting to announce such a purpose. After all, any group of Christians, even gathered across denominational lines, could quickly formulate a definition of themselves that all of them could agree on. It would go something like this: Christians are people who acknowledge Jesus Christ as he is known in the Bible as their Lord and Savior and seek in the company of fellow Christians to live by his promises and obey his commands. But ask what Christians should think and say and do about any of the controversial theological and ethical issues of our time, and it becomes immediately clear that although we may define ourselves the same way, we do *not* agree on what it means to be a Christian. What should Christians think and say and do, for instance, about evangelism and missions? Economic justice and its implications for capitalism and socialism? The place of women in church and society? The meaning of "salvation"? Social welfare? Nuclear armament and peacemaking? Prayer in public schools? Abortion? Capital punishment? Homosexuality? The attitude of Christians toward other religions? The foreign policy of our nation? Ask any of these questions and Christians choose up sides, get red in the face, and either yell at each other or refuse to talk together at all. And the result is not only that the Christian cause suffers but, even worse, that the world suffers—a world that already knows all about suspicion, hostility, and warfare between rival groups and desperately needs a clear and consistent witness to the reconciling and renewing work of God in Jesus Christ.

I hope in this book to help us Christians and our churches understand and overcome this contradiction between our theoretical unity and our often bitter practical disunity. I am convinced that we cannot achieve this goal if we begin with particular issues like those I have mentioned. More often than not, such an approach only emphasizes our differences. We must rather begin with a more fundamental question: *Why* is it that people who read the same Bible and talk about the same Christ, even when they belong to the same church, have so much trouble getting along with each other and committing themselves to a common Christian witness in the world?

I believe the answer is obvious. Before we even open a Bible, reflect on the significance of Christ, listen to a sermon, or enter into conversation about what Christians or the church should say and do, we all bring with us some conscious or unconscious presuppositions about the meaning of Christian faith and life that determine what we are able and willing —and unable and unwilling—to hear from scripture, from fellow Christians, or even from God.

This understanding of the root of our disagreements suggests a line of thought that could help us resolve them. If we could identify and clarify these presuppositions, we might at the very least understand a little better those Christians who are different from us. And if we could agree on some criteria that enable us to evaluate both the strengths and the weaknesses of the theological and ethical conclusions that follow from these different presuppositions, we might even *learn* something from each other, come a little closer to a genuine consensus about what it means to be a Christian, and be equipped to make a little more unified and faithful witness to the common Lord we all confess.

This line of thought leads to the agenda for this book. In Part I we will briefly identify four types of Christianity that express the expectations and demands of different types of Christians as they read the Bible, think about Christ, and decide how (or whether!) to participate in the life of the church. We will suggest some criteria for evaluating these types of Christianity. Next, using the criteria, we will devote a chapter to each type, evaluating both its strengths and its weaknesses. Then, in Part II, we will outline a view of Christian faith and life that attempts to incorporate the strengths and avoid the weaknesses of each of the four types in order to formulate an understanding of what it means to be a Christian that could unite divided Christians and prepare them to be agents of

God's reconciling work in Jesus Christ in and for a tragically and ominously divided world.

I realize that I have set an unrealistic goal for myself. If it could be done, others would already have done it. But if this book helps us to make only a little progress toward the goal, I will be satisfied.

Part I
Some Old Songs

Christian Orthodoxy,
Liberalism, and Pietism

In preparation for this part of our study, we need first to introduce the types of Christianity we will discuss and then to identify the criteria we will use to evaluate them.

The Types

We have suggested that it is not difficult to get Christians to formulate a definition of what a Christian is that they can all agree on. Nevertheless, when one first asks any group of Christians (in the United States at least) what it means to be a Christian, one is likely to get four kinds of answers: (1) Some will answer first in terms of what Christians believe and will define Christianity in terms of their convictions about the correct content of Christian faith. (2) Some will speak about the claim of God on individual Christians' lives and will define Christianity in terms of personal Christian morality. (3) Others will think first of commitment to the political and economic justice of the kingdom of God and will define Christianity in terms of Christian social activism. (4) Still others will bear witness to their personal experience of the grace of God in Jesus Christ and will define Christianity in terms of being saved and enjoying the benefits of their salvation.

These answers do not necessarily contradict each other. Most Christians might agree that all of them need to be incorporated into a complete definition of a Christian. But these answers do represent different presuppositions about the fundamental message of the Bible, the significance of Christ, and the meaning of Christian faith and life. They lead to different priorities. They result in tensions among Christians even when they reach theoretical agreement about who they are. They indicate that we do not always mean the same thing even when we say the same thing. I believe in fact that these different answers represent different types of Christianity that cause deep divisions among individual Christians and groups of Christians, even when these divisions are covered over with nice-sounding consensus statements. It is the four types of Christianity represented by these four kinds of answers that will concern us in the following chapters.

It is possible to identify other ways of talking about what it means to be a Christian and other ways of categorizing types of Christians (H. Richard Niebuhr's way of doing it, for instance, in his classic *Christ and Culture*). But I have chosen these four ways because I believe that in one form or another they are the most common options that both unite and divide individual Christians and groups of Christians in our time (again, at least in the United States). All four answers we listed are common in the mainline denominations and in many of their individual congregations. Indeed, many Christians and Christian groups identify themselves more by their commitment to one of these types of Christianity than by their commitment to their denomination and feel more at home with like-minded Christians in other denominations than with different types of Christians in their own. We work with this way of distinguishing Christians, therefore, because we believe that the struggle that goes on in the everyday life of the church to understand and stand for authentic Christian faith and life is best understood as the struggle between the assumptions, claims, and priorities of these four fundamental options.

In order to demonstrate that these types are all alive and well, not just as abstract theological positions but as expressions of our experiential understanding of—or confusion about—what it means to be a Christian, we will discuss them as they are expressed in hymns that are often sung during worship in many of our churches. But we will also study them in the context of some movements in the history of Christian thought that have technical theological names. "Faith of Our Fathers" (chapter 1) represents a theological movement called "orthodoxy." "They'll Know We Are Christians by Our Love" (chapter 2) and "Rise Up, O Men of God" (chapter 3) represents two versions of the theological movement called "liberalism." "Amazing Grace" (chapter 4) represents what is called "pietism."

Although orthodoxy, liberalism, and pietism have precise meanings in the history of Christian theology, they are slippery words in everyday theological conversation. They mean different things to different people and are often used only as a means of complimentary or derogatory name-calling. It could be argued that we should avoid them altogether because they confuse rather than clarify theological discussion and impede the quest for Christian unity. But to avoid them would be to avoid terms that are inevitably used both by lay people and by ministers to categorize themselves and other Christians. Self-understanding and mutual understanding could be furthered, real differences among us clarified, and unnecessary differences overcome if we could understand and use these theological categories with their precise historical meaning. That is what we will try to do. As we take up each of the types of Christianity, we will briefly describe its place in the history of theology (especially Protestant theology) and use its appropriate theological title as we evaluate it. Those who are interested in a more detailed study of these movements than we can develop here will find a list of suggested readings at the end of the book.

Criteria for Evaluation

In light of what we have said about the presuppositions we all bring with us when we think about what it means to believe and live as Christians, it might seem at first glance that it would be impossible for us to agree on any criteria for evaluating the strengths and weaknesses of the types of Christianity we will consider. It might seem that all we can do is describe the preferences or "points of view" of different kinds of Christians and groups of Christians. But the situation is not as hopeless as it appears at first sight. There are some general principles of evaluation that all four types of Christians should be able to agree on. Following are four such criteria we will use.

1. *We must listen to* all *of what scripture tells us about the meaning of Christian faith and life.* We must pay attention especially to those passages that call into question or conflict with what we would *like* the Bible to say or think that it *must* or *should* say. If we listen only to those parts of scripture we find congenial, we do not listen at all. We only use the Bible to confirm what we think we already know. If we really want to overcome our own presuppositions and biases and correct those of others, we have to subject them to critical examination in light of the *whole* biblical witness to the word and work and will of God in Jesus Christ.

2. *We must listen with respect to other Christians and to the church, both in the past and in the present.* It is very difficult for any individual Christian or group of Christians to be aware, much less critical, of their own limitations, prejudices, and presuppositions in interpreting scripture. One way to allow them to be exposed and corrected is to listen to how other Christians and the whole community of Christians have interpreted it in the past and interpret it in the present.

This statement bristles with problems, of course. Other Christians have their own limitations, prejudices, and presuppositions that blind them to what scripture teaches. "The church" is in fact not one church but many churches, different denominations and congregations within them that often disagree in their convictions about what it means to be a Christian. Even when there is a consensus within and among these churches, the consensus itself could be mistaken or inadequate; what churches as well as individual Christians are able and willing to hear from scripture is limited by all sorts of psychological, political, historical, and sociological factors. Sometimes an individual Christian (a Martin Luther!), with a few like-minded Christians, may see some aspect of Christian faith and life that the whole church has overlooked, forgotten, or refused to acknowledge.

Nevertheless, despite all these difficulties, we are more likely to be able to discern the word of God for Christian faith and life when we are willing to seek it, not alone, or only in the company of others who are our "type" of Christian, but (a) in openness to learn from other individual Christians who have gone before us and who live around us, (b) in openness to learn from the local congregation and larger denomination to which we belong, and (c) in openness to learn from other Christian traditions, all of which (even in the disagreements and tensions among them) make up the "one holy catholic church" all Christians should be able to confess together.

Most Christians enter into this conversation committed especially to the biblical interpretation and theological and ethical teaching of some particular Christian tradition. It will become clear that I am committed to the Reformed Presbyterian tradition, with its roots especially in the thought of John Calvin. I want to emphasize my conviction, however, that to follow in this tradition is by definition to be committed to the authority of Jesus Christ as he is known in scripture over *all* church traditions, including my own. It is to be eager and willing to let every type of Christianity—orthodox, liberal, and pietistic—be corrected by the Word of God. It is gladly to enter into conversation with and learn from all Christian traditions in order that we may learn together not just what some theologian or church wills but what God wills that we Christians should believe and do.

3. *We must listen with respect to other Christians who are sexually, racially, economically, politically, and culturally different from us.* Individual Christians, groups of Christians, and indeed whole churches have trouble reaching consensus on the meaning of Christian faith and life because (often unconsciously) we all read into scripture and bring into the church the biases, prejudices, and self-interest of our particular sex, race, class, region, political affiliation, and cultural environment. The result is that theological conflicts are often only the external manifesta-

tion of a hidden conflict between groups that are in the majority, and have power, and those that are in the minority, and are powerless. This does not have to be the case, however. Christians who are different from each other in these ways can prove the seriousness of their quest to learn what authentic Christian faith and life are by their willingness to talk and listen to each other and be instructed and corrected by each other. According to the scripture all Christians seek to interpret and live by, to be a Christian means by definition to belong to a reconciled and reconciling community in which all kinds of people who are otherwise strangers or enemies learn to know and care about each other, live together in justice and peace, and understand themselves as a people called to be agents of God's justice and reconciliation in the world. The strengths and weaknesses of all types of Christianity are to be evaluated in light of this biblical view of Christian faith and life.

4. *We must evaluate every interpretation of Christian faith and life in light of its own declared intentions.* Is it developed logically? Does it have inner consistency? Does it achieve its own goals? This principle of evaluation does not in itself help us to judge the truth of any type of Christianity. But it can help us to see how some weaknesses of the various types could be corrected without rejecting but, in fact, maintaining what is important to them.

All these criteria for evaluating the four types of Christianity we are about to consider are more complex than our brief statement of them suggests. I hope that the use we make of them will clarify and demonstrate their validity and relevance.

One last word before we begin. As I have discussed these types of Christianity with numerous groups of lay people and ministers, the results have always been the same. (1) Most people are reluctant to identify themselves with any one type; they recognize something of themselves in them all. (2) Most people have less trouble identifying *other* Christians they know, or know about, with one or another of the types. (3) Some people think I have misunderstood and unfairly criticized one or another of the types and tend to be defensive and even angry when they hear what I say about it. (4) This is usually a good sign that it is with this type they feel most at home! (5) Real learning takes place when people begin to think critically about their own as well as about others' understanding of what it means to be a Christian.

1
Faith of Our Fathers

Faith of our fathers! living still
In spite of dungeon, fire, and sword,
O how our hearts beat high with joy
Whene'er we hear that glorious word:
Faith of our fathers, holy faith!
We will be true to thee till death.

What does it mean to be a Christian? It means to accept and defend the faith formulated for us by our "fathers" in the past and preserved and handed down to us by those who have followed after them. (The hymn was written before we learned to acknowledge the fact that "mothers" also had something to do with shaping, preserving, and handing down the faith we have received.) All other aspects of Christian faith and life depend on knowing, accepting, and being faithful to the truth of Christianity as faithful Christians before us have defined it. Christians are first and foremost true believers. Genuine Christianity is therefore *orthodox* (right-thinking) Christianity.

The history of the Christian movement is to a large extent the history of debate about what truly orthodox Christianity is—and the history of the division of Christians into different groups, each of which claims that the particular theological teachers and tradition that have shaped their faith are the genuinely orthodox ones. Some churches (such as the Roman Catholic, Eastern Orthodox, Lutheran, Presbyterian and Reformed, and, to some extent, the Anglican, Episcopal, and Methodist churches) have formulated confessional and creedal statements to give official status to their version of orthodoxy. Some Protestant churches (most notably the Baptist churches) have no official doctrinal statements but nevertheless are firmly convinced that theirs is the true orthodoxy. There are also nondenominational groups that identify themselves with no church tradition yet claim that they are the only real defenders of orthodox Christianity.

This multiplicity of orthodoxies is not quite as chaotic as it seems at first glance. All Christians agree that the original fathers and mothers of the faith are those we meet in the Old and New Testaments and have in common their acknowledgment of the authority of scripture. Even though they are divided into many denominations and factions within and across denominational lines, most Christians who call themselves orthodox share a broad agreement about the basic content of true Christian faith. They accept what the ancient creeds of Nicaea (A.D. 325) and Chalcedon (A.D. 451) teach about the deity and humanity of Christ. They accept officially or unofficially the summary of the Christian faith in the Apostles' Creed, with its trinitarian affirmation of the creative, redemptive, and transforming work of God the Father, Son, and Holy Spirit. Despite many conflicting claims about the details of the faith, they share some common affirmations that make it possible at least in a general way to speak not only of Roman Catholic or Eastern Orthodox or this or that version of Protestant orthodoxy but of "Christian" orthodoxy.

Our purpose in this chapter, however, is not to enter into the debate about whose orthodoxy is truly orthodox. Nor is it to try to define in a systematic way the content of a true orthodoxy underlying or transcending all the various claims to orthodoxy. Our concern is rather to evaluate the orthodox *mentality*— to discuss the extent to which the meaning of Christian faith and life can be defined in terms of *any* version of orthodox belief. Because this book is written by a theologian in the Presbyterian and Reformed tradition, and because it is better to criticize one's own tradition before one begins to criticize other traditions, we will emphasize what various versions of Protestant orthodoxy have in common: the conviction that Christian truth is above all biblical truth, the conviction that to be a true Christian is to be above all a Bible-believing Christian, the conviction that no theology, church tradition, or confessional statement is acceptable unless it is biblically defensible.

In Defense of Christian Orthodoxy

For many people today any kind of religious orthodoxy, Christian as well as non-Christian, suggests a long list of bad things: intolerance, bigotry, narrow-mindedness, intellectual arrogance, outdatedness, irrelevance, and (when opportunity is given) the tendency to repress and oppress "unbelievers." We shall see that there is good reason for such suspicion. But there are also some good things to be said for Christian orthodoxy (as for other forms of religious orthodoxy, though they do not concern us here).

Orthodoxy and the Bible

Orthodox Christians, especially in Protestant forms, insist that to be a real Christian is to know, accept, understand, and defend the truth—the *objective* truth—concerning God, the world, and human life as it is given in scripture and preserved in Christian tradition. The great strength of this orthodox emphasis on objective truth is that it is biblical. The biblical writers do not write to tell us only about their subjective personal feelings, intuitions, opinions, "creative" insights, and reflections concerning God. They do not ask us to believe what they say because they are deeply religious people who are sensitive to the "spiritual dimension of life" (some were and some were not). They do not argue that what they proclaim should be accepted because they sincerely believe it, or because it has meant so much to them personally, or because of what admirable people they have become as a result of their faith. They do not proclaim themselves and their own wisdom, piety, personal experience, faith, or exemplary lives. Nor do they proclaim truth that is true only if and when it is understood, believed, experienced, and lived out. What they proclaim is truth that they believe is true *in itself,* truth for all people, whether or not they know about it, acknowledge it, serve and benefit from it. It is the truth about a God who is not one of many gods people may choose according to their personal taste and inclination but a God who is the one living and true God, the only God there is. It is truth about a Lord and Savior who is not just *a* way but *the* way, not just a light that enlightens Christians but the true light that enlightens everyone (John 1:9), the light of the whole world (John 8:12).

Neither in scripture nor in orthodox Christianity does insistence on this objective truth of God and God's self-revelation in Christ mean that our subjective response to the truth is unimportant. On the contrary, just because this truth is the ultimate truth about the origin, meaning, and goal of human life, it is essential that people hear, accept, understand, and live by it. Nevertheless, it is not any aspect of our subjective response that makes the truth to be true. It *is* true. The subjective element is *response* to the truth, not that which makes it to be true.

Any view of what it means to be a Christian that is faithful to the biblical view must include the courage of orthodoxy to claim that biblical truth is not just "our" truth but *the* truth, not just truth for us Christians but truth for everyone, not just a matter of subjective perception and preference but a matter of *objective* truth.

Orthodoxy and the Church

Fights over the content of truly orthodox interpretation of biblical truth
have split the church into enemy camps. Christian unity, love, discipleship, mission, and service have been sacrificed because of some Christians' stubborn insistence on the infallibility of some particular confessional definition of Christian truth. But in order to see the importance
of orthodoxy's preoccupation with the issue of truth, we have only to see
what happens when the church ignores it.

If it is not commitment to biblical-Christian truth, then it will be
commitment to something else that provides the motivation and purpose
of the church. It may be commitment to this or that preacher with great
personal charm, rhetorical skill, or administrative ability. It may be
loyalty to an old or new ecclesiastical structure with its officials, manuals
of operation, rules and regulations, policies and programs, and obsession
with discovering the right process of priority setting or decision making.
It may be allowing what a church says and does to be determined by the
religious, economic, political, racial, or cultural preferences of the majority of church members. It may be seeking the meaning and purpose of
the church in dignified traditional liturgy or in "creative" contemporary
worship. It may be centering the life of the church in Christian "fellowship" with family night suppers and programs and activities for children,
young people, singles, couples, senior citizens, business men and women,
homemakers, and so on. It may be making the church into a center for
"personal growth," using psychological insights and skills to nurture
emotional health and happiness and develop people's capacity for "interpersonal relationships." It may mean deliberately or unconsciously "letting the world set the agenda" by organizing interest groups and task
forces to support various liberal or conservative political and economic
causes.

Now, none of these emphases are wrong in themselves. But as soon
as the church no longer seeks its basis, meaning, and goal in biblical-
Christian truth, it idolatrously replaces faith and hope in God with faith
and hope in church leaders, church structures, liturgical rituals, or to-
getherness for their own sake. It becomes indistinguishable from other
organizations and movements that can do just as good a job or better of
edifying, inspiring, entertaining, and helping people and improving the
world. Both the integrity and the real relevance of the church's ministry
depend on its testing everything it says and does by asking the question
of orthodox Christians: Is it allowed or required by biblical-Christian
faith as it is preserved in the theological standards of the church? What
does faithfulness to scripture and Christian tradition require us to say
and do—and leave unsaid and undone?

Orthodoxy and Personal Experience

Orthodox Christianity is often criticized for not paying enough attention to the important role of personal experience in what people can and should believe about God and human life in the world. It is accused of demanding that Christians accept correct theological ideas and doctrines even when they are contradicted by personal experience. This criticism is often justified. But two things can be said for orthodoxy in response to this criticism.

In the first place, it is a *strength* of orthodox Christians that they believe even when their personal experience calls their faith into question. When we are happy and healthy, prosperous and successful, and when justice and peace and plenty for all seem at least possible in the world—then it is easy to confess faith in a powerful and loving God who is present and at work in the world. Experience seems to justify such faith. But orthodox Christians have been able to make this confession also in the face of their own and their loved ones' sickness, suffering, and death and in spite of the never-ending suffering, poverty, injustice, and oppression in the world around them. Their faith in the power and love of God has comforted them and enabled them to continue to trust in God even when others have understandably concluded in despair that God does not exist or that God must be either a loving God who is not powerful enough to do anything about human misery or a powerful God who is not loving enough to do anything about it. Their faith has also given some orthodox Christians the courage and strength to keep up the struggle for justice and peace even when others have understandably given up and withdrawn from the battle. Faith that stubbornly persists *nevertheless* in believing in the rule of an almighty and loving God despite experiential evidence to the contrary must be recognized as a strength of orthodox Christians.

Second, it must be pointed out that in its original and most authentic form Christian orthodoxy is not built on faith *in spite of* personal experience but on faith *in light of* personal experience. The story of the Old Testament is the story of how the ancient Jews experienced God's guidance and care for them and through them for all people. The New Testament is the story of what we have heard, seen with our own eyes, "looked upon and touched with our hands" (1 John 1:1)—the story of the love and power of God that the first Christians actually *experienced* in Jesus Christ.

The story of the Old and New Testaments is a believing interpretation of history, but it is nevertheless an interpretation of *history*, not just a made-up story. It is of course the story of what some other people experienced in the distant past and not of what we ourselves have experienced. But Christians recognize "those" people as our people, their God as our God, their history as the history of where we come from. The biblical story is an *unfinished* story, the story of the continuing presence of evil, suffering, and death in the world, the story of the promised victory of God's justice and love that will be completely fulfilled only in the future. But it is a story that proclaims a hope for the future that is based not just on wishful thinking but on what God has already begun to accomplish and what we have already experienced in human history.

Orthodox Christianity does not have to be the kind of orthodoxy that ignores and contradicts present human experience. It can be an orthodoxy that interprets present human experience in light of the memory of what God has already done in past human experience and in light of the sure hope for what he will do in future human experience.

Orthodoxy and Secular Society

The history of the public influence of Christian orthodoxy has not been a happy one. Convinced that they alone have the truth about God and human life in the world, various groups of Christians have tried to impose their truth on each other. Bloody wars have been fought and hundreds of thousands of people slaughtered in the name of true faith in Christ. Christians have tortured and killed non-Christians and fellow Christians in order to achieve the rule of the "true faith" over the Christian *and* over the civil community. In our time, there are orthodox Christians who try to impose their orthodoxy on others by less violent means. They impugn the integrity of individual people and groups who think and live differently from them. They try openly or underhandedly to keep Jews, other non-Christians, and even other Christians who are not like them from moving into their neighborhood, joining their clubs, enjoying the same business opportunities they enjoy. They seek political leadership and public policies that not only protect but are partial to their particular version of true Christian faith and life. They try to get enough popular support to enact laws that require everyone to conform to their own religious beliefs and practices or be rejected, excluded, and even deprived of civil rights.

In light of this history it is not surprising that most modern societies have declared themselves religiously neutral. Religion has become a private affair. Most of us now believe that people of different faiths have the right to their personal beliefs but not the right to enforce others to live by them. Most people have learned to be tolerant of others with different religious and moral convictions, not only because of laws that require the separation of church and state but also because they are genuinely convinced that all people should have the freedom to believe or not believe whatever they choose, so long as they do not infringe on the rights of others or disturb generally accepted standards of public order and decency. Modern civilized societies, therefore, have become pluralistic societies in which the Christian faith is recognized as one option among others. Tolerance has become for many people the supreme virtue even when it is not practiced. Anyone who claims to have *the* truth or *the* right way of life is considered narrow-minded and dangerous. The time is past when any version of Christian orthodoxy can be imposed on governments and societies—except in a few places, for short periods of time, when some reactionary individuals and groups manage to gain temporary control. And most people, including most Christians, are glad they can live in a tolerant, pluralistic society free from the hatred, bigotry, and injustice that tears any society apart when "true believers" try to take over.

But we have paid a high price for our religious tolerance and pluralism. What most threatens the order and cohesion of many modern societies, including our own, is no longer the conflict between various versions of orthodoxy. It is the tendency to believe that there *is* no truth but only personal preferences and private opinions, each of which is just as good as any other so long as it is sincerely believed. The result, as many nonreligious as well as religious observers have noted, is that we live in a society in which there are no longer any commonly accepted goals or values or paths of effective action. There is no consensus, for instance, about how sexual and familial relationships should be ordered. Public relations and selling techniques have often replaced commitment to honesty and excellence in business and professional life and even in government. Vision of the common good has been replaced by concern for what is good for *me,* what makes *me* happy, what gives *me* security and personal fulfillment, or what enables *me* to be saved. Many people (perhaps especially young people who are less and less taught the traditional values and goals their parents remember and theoretically acknowledge) simply drift from day to day, moved by the whims and pleasures of the moment or by whatever happens to be the latest psychological, political, religious, artistic, or health fad. The rootlessness, chaos, and narcissism that come when "tolerant" people believe that there is no truth applicable to all are just as personally and socially destructive as the authoritarianism and intolerance of the old competing orthodoxies, with their claim to have the truth that should be imposed on all.[1]

For the sake of its own survival, modern society needs Christians who believe that there *is* a true understanding of the meaning and goal of human individual and communal life. It needs Christians who believe that they know where this truth is to be found and who openly recommend it to others. It needs *orthodox* Christians. It does not of course need Christians who destroy the hard-won advantages of tolerance and freedom of (or from) religion by trying to force others to think and live as they do. But it does need Christians who believe that they know the way in a lost and disintegrating world and dare to point it out to others as the right way.

Why should we not freely and openly advocate Christian truth and the Christian way in the public arena? In every area of life other than the religious we *expect* people to defend the points of view to which they are deeply committed. It is not considered "intolerant" for sports fans to claim that their team is the best. Lovers of Bach or rock do not hesitate to defend their musical taste as superior. No one protests the right of Republicans or Democrats vigorously to defend their political views as the right ones. We *expect* advocates of capitalism and socialism to argue long and hard for their economic philosophies. Why should not the religious question of the fundamental meaning and purpose of human life be open to the same passionate advocacy as questions from other areas of life?

Orthodox Christians do not have to be Christians who try to force others in our pluralistic society to think like Christians, pray like Christians, live like Christians. (A forced Christian is not a Christian at all.) But they can be Christians who by the way they live and talk about their faith recommend it to others as not only the truth but the good news it is—good news for *all* people. They can be Christians who work in the public sphere for government and social institutions that reflect the justice and compassion and truth of the God to whom they are committed, not just for the sake of the success of their version of Christianity but for the common welfare of all humanity. Such orthodox Christians are not a threat to a tolerant pluralistic society; such a society desperately needs them.

Criticism of Christian Orthodoxy

Having defended the merits of the orthodox version of what it means to be a Christian, we now turn to its weaknesses. In general our criticism will be that the fundamental problem with orthodoxy is that it is not orthodox enough. Orthodox Christians tend to forget some things they should have learned from the very scripture and tradition they themselves are so rightly concerned to preserve and defend.

Orthodox Theology and Everyday Life

We have defended Christian orthodoxy against the charge that it is irrelevant to everyday human experience. But the charge is not without justification. It is true that orthodox faith gives Christians courage and hope to believe in God's powerful love and justice even when they experience only the silence or absence of God. It is true that orthodoxy is based on the experience of God's word and deed in the past history of God's people. But perhaps the weakness behind everything else that can be said in criticism of orthodoxy is its tendency actually to contribute to the sense of the absence or silence of God in our *present* lives, here and now. This weakness and its consequences become apparent when we look at the orthodox understanding of the nature of God, the meaning of faith, and Christian ethics.

The nature of God. Orthodox Christians want above all to preserve and defend the truth of the Christian faith as it is given in scripture. But what is that truth? Biblical truth is personal-historical truth, truth about a living God who like a father, mother, judge, shepherd, or ruler is continually at work helping God's people on their way. It is supremely the truth about the God who in the earthly Jesus once dwelt, and in the risen Christ still dwells, among us as our friend, companion, guide, and liberator.

Orthodox Christianity on the other hand tends to turn the living, speaking, acting God of the Bible into the idea of a great impersonal Supreme Being. Using many big adjectives, it can give elaborate definitions of God without any reference to the revelatory words and deeds of God in the history of Israel and in Jesus Christ.[2] Even when with happy inconsistency it does go on to speak about the work of God in human history and experience, it tends to think of God as an infinite, unchanging, eternal "transcendent" God who is above the world, determining and controlling everything that happens in it from the heavenly heights but personally uninvolved in human affairs, unlimited but also untouched and unmoved by all creaturely limitations, feelings, and experiences. Even when orthodox theology comes to speak of God in Christ, it sees the "divine nature" of Christ in his majestic power and authority over us, and only the "human nature" of Christ in the self-giving love that leads him to stand with and for us in our creaturely and sinful neediness. The human Jesus may be present with us as our friend and companion in the concrete experiences of our everyday lives, but God is above all that, especially when those experiences involve weakness, failure, sin, suffering, and death. The God of orthodoxy is by definition a distant God, who is not only unwilling but unable to be present in a world and in lives that are so ungodlike.

In short, while orthodox Christianity wants above all to defend the truth and authority of scripture, its concept of God as the highest and purest *idea* of God, and its understanding of what such a God can and cannot do, prevents it from understanding what the God of the Bible actually does and promises to do: demonstrate infinite divine *power* as the infinite divine *love* that makes God willing and able to be in as well as above the world, to be truly human as well as truly divine, to be the compassionate friend as well as the stern judge of guilty sinners, to share as well as overcome the frailty, pain, injustice, and death that destroy human lives in the world as we experience it.

Faith. The difference between the biblical and the orthodox doctrine of God leads to a corresponding difference between their understanding of what it means to have faith in God. In the Bible (and in the theology of the Protestant Reformers)[3] faith is primarily *trust,* the grateful and obedient acknowledgment of the ordering and helping presence of God in our lives. For orthodox Christians, on the other hand, faith tends to be *belief,* intellectual acceptance of correct doctrinal statements about God or Christ. Of course, orthodox Christians also believe that Christian faith is faith in the God or the Christ we come to know in scripture. But what concerns them most is a correct theology of the inspiration and authority of scripture as such and the church's traditional interpretation of what it teaches about such doctrines as the virgin birth, substitutionary atonement, bodily resurrection, and Second Coming. In orthodox theology, faith tends subtly to become not so much a personal attitude of trust and thankful response as a kind of right thinking. As a result, biblical confidence in the saving power of God tends to become confidence in Christians' ability to save themselves by the power of their "saving faith" in orthodox doctrine.

The Christian life. According to the Bible, to live by faith means to remember what God has said and done in the past, to seek in every new time, place, and situation to discern the new things God is saying and doing in the present, and to live in anticipation of more new things God will say and do in fulfilling God's promise of a new creation and a new humanity. To live by faith is therefore to be open continually to learn afresh what *we* have to say and do in every new time, place, and situation in order to live in thankful obedience to this living God.

Orthodox theology, on the other hand, is suspicious of such talk. Because of its concern to preserve and defend the truth of past revelation, it is suspicious of any thought of "new" revelation and of the idea that changing circumstances could have any influence on proper Christian action. Orthodox Christians seek to know the unchangeable will of the unchangeable God that tells Christians what they are always to do in every time, place, and situation. And they believe they can arrive at such knowledge (1) by applying general biblical and theological "principles" of ethical behavior to concrete personal and social problems, (2) by "logical deduction" from the "eternal truths" and "enduring moral absolutes" once and for all revealed by the "propositional revelation" given in scripture, or (3) by rational analysis of the "natural laws" built into the "order of creation" when God created the world. This way of seeking the will of God leads to the ethical, political, and social conservatism typical of orthodox Christians. They tend to be exclusively past-oriented (holding on to what they believe to be the God-ordained permanent moral and social order valid for all times) rather than present- or future-oriented (open to God's guidance in seeking fresh solutions to ethical problems and working for a new social order).

Two things should be said in evaluation of this orthodox ethic, the first concerning the way it confirms what we have already said about its doctrine of God and the second concerning its need to guard against ethical subjectivism and relativism.

In the first place, we may heartily agree with the insistence of orthodox Christianity that God is not a self-contradictory, arbitrary God who wills and commands one thing today and something quite different tomorrow. The God of the Bible and God's will for human life are indeed the same yesterday, today, and tomorrow in the sense that in all the particular things God requires in different situations, God is always faithful to God's loving and just nature and purposes that never change. But to the extent that orthodox Christians try to discover the will of God by rational deduction from timeless ethical principles and general moral laws (even those derived from scripture), they defeat their own good intentions. They imply that while once a long time ago (at the creation of the world or in "Bible times" or perhaps centuries ago when orthodox confessional statements were first formulated) God may have spoken and acted in human history to help people know how to live, now God has retired in silence and inactivity from human history. We can no longer learn from God but have to tell ourselves what we have to say and do as we try to discover as best we can the concrete implications of the abstract moral principles, general truths, and "natural laws" that have taken the place of the living God as our source of ethical guidance. In theory, orthodox Christians may acknowledge their need for the continuing guidance of the Holy Spirit in making ethical decisions, but in practice they tend to assume that the Holy Spirit will not and cannot contradict what they think they already know by applying their rationalistic and legalistic method for discovering the unchangeable will of God. To the extent that they live by such an ethic, orthodox Christians make themselves vulnerable to the charge that at least in present human experience their God is a silent and absentee God. They also deprive themselves of the good news that is at the heart of their own Bible: God not only was and will be but is a living, acting, speaking God, a God who does not leave us alone to figure out for ourselves how we should live, a God whom we can count on to be present with us, here and now, to help and guide us in *our* time and place with the particular questions, problems, and decisions *we* face.

A second criticism of the ethics of Christian orthodoxy: We may heartily agree that it is rightly opposed to the "subjectivism" and "ethical relativism" of a "situation ethic" that all too easily enables people to justify doing whatever seems desirable in their own eyes by saying that they believe it is the will of God for them in their particular situation. But their understanding of Christian ethics makes orthodox Christians vulnerable to the very subjectivism and relativism they reject. History is full of examples of how easy it is for Bible-believing orthodox Christians to confuse their own personal prejudices or those of their particular racial, political, economic, or national group with the "eternal truths," "biblical principles," or "moral absolutes" they think they have derived from scripture and from the order of creation. In the past some orthodox Christians protested the rise of modern democracy because they were sure that various forms of repressive authoritarianism were "God willed" and "natural." In the name of God, the Bible, and the "laws of nature" they supported slavery against those who believed that all people are created equal. In our time, using the same kind of biblical and theological arguments, some orthodox Christians have sought to maintain the inferior status of women in church and society, supported racial apartheid, and defended oppressive economic, political, and miliary systems. In both past and present, some orthodox Christians have condemned new scientific discoveries and advances as "atheistic." To the extent that they close themselves to the living God who promises to speak a surprising new word and do revolutionary new things in every new time and place, they have no guard against substituting their own conservative wishes and opinions for the truth of God they most sincerely want to serve.

In other words, precisely when we share the goal of orthodox Christians to obey the will of God we come to know in scripture, we must do a better job of it than they. Our objection to them is not that they are too orthodox but that they are not orthodox enough.

Orthodoxy and the Church

We said in our defense of orthodox Christianity that the church needs its insistence on commitment to biblical and theological truth. But there are some tendencies in orthodoxy that work against the very biblical and theological integrity of the church it is so anxious to preserve.

Tendency to neglect the mission of the church in the world. According to classical Protestant definition, the marks of a truly Christian church are the pure preaching of the Word of God and the right administration of the sacraments (with church discipline sometimes added). Emphasis on Word and sacrament is indeed indispensable for a biblical doctrine of the church, but this definition speaks only of what happens within the church for the benefit of church members. Totally lacking in classical definitions of the church is the biblical emphasis on the people of God called to be a "light to the nations," sent out to serve the kingdom of God or to be God's agents of reconciliation and renewal in the world.

Orthodox Christians have of course always been interested in the world. But (in contrast to the Reformers themselves)[4] their concern has tended to be not so much for the sake of the world as for the sake of the church itself. For them political authorities are there not so much to preserve freedom and order for the sake of the common good of all as to preserve freedom and order only for the sake of the church's preaching and worship—and sometimes to impose the orthodox understanding of Christian faith and life on everyone. The wisdom and achievements of secular culture are viewed with suspicion as something to be resisted and officially replaced with orthodox Christian ideas and practices. Even when orthodox Christians become interested in evangelism and missions, their purpose is often not to equip people to go *into* the world so that God's loving and just will may be done on earth as it is in heaven; their purpose has often been to invite people *out* of the world to receive the comfort, help, and salvation offered true believers in the church.

To the extent that orthodox Christians believe the world exists for the sake of the church rather than the church for the sake of the world, it fails to understand what according to scripture is the purpose of the very true preaching of the Word and right administration of the sacraments it seeks to serve.

Tendency to destroy the unity of the church. Orthodox Christians rightly seek the unity of the church in common commitment to the truth made known in scripture and preserved by Christian tradition. But against their own good intentions they have often been the cause of division and separations in the church. The reason for the contradiction between the unity they seek and the divisiveness this often causes is their tendency to confuse biblical-theological truth with what they consider to be the only correct interpretation of it by some individual theologian, theological movement, or confessional tradition. In conversation with fellow Christians who interpret scripture differently or who have learned from different church traditions, orthodox Christians tend to assume that unity can be achieved only when "they" are willing to agree with "us." And when their opponents cannot be persuaded (or perhaps forced) to do so, orthodox Christians tend to accuse them of disagreeing not with one interpretation of scripture but with *God* and to argue that it is "they," not "we," who are guilty of destroying the unity of the church.

Such an attitude blocks the very unity-in-truth that orthodox Christians seek in at least three ways.

In the first place, Christians who understand Christian unity as doctrinal conformity with their way of thinking tend in fact to be less concerned about the unity that comes with common faithfulness to authentic biblical-Christian truth than about the victory of their own theological position or party and the defeat of other Christians who are considered to be not brothers and sisters in Christ but "the enemy."

Second, such Christians misunderstand what their own Bible teaches about the nature of true Christian unity. According to scripture, Christians are united not by their commitment to one *theology* but by their commitment to one *Lord,* one *Spirit,* one *God and Father of us all* (1 Cor. 12:4–13; Eph. 4:4–6). The New Testament does not, of course, teach a wide-open tolerance that allows individual Christians and groups of Christians to think and do anything they please. It gives theological criteria by which Christians and churches are to examine both others and themselves to determine whether they are in fact worshiping and serving the one true God or false gods. It knows that there are expressions of Christian faith and life (including some that claim to be orthodox) that destroy rather than enrich the body. Nevertheless, the New Testament writers teach—and precisely in their differences from one another demonstrate—that true Christian unity is based on faith in the same God and not on faith in the same theology.

Third, Christians who confuse their interpretation of Christian truth with the truth itself cut themselves off from the knowledge of the very truth they rightly believe to be the ground of genuine Christian unity. How can they know and defend the truth if they are unwilling to grant that they themselves, as well as others, may need to change their views in light of biblical teaching? This brings us to a final weakness of orthodox Christianity that may be the one weakness that lies behind all the others we have discussed.

The Self-confidence of Orthodoxy

Orthodox Christians know too much. They know too much, too certainly, about what God can and must—and cannot and must not—be and do and say. They know too much, too certainly, about what the will of God is for human life in every situation. They also know too much, too certainly, about what scientific and historical truth concerning the structures and processes of God's created world can and cannot be. Their theology is admirable in its courageous faith, completeness, and logical consistency, but not notably marked by any inclination to stand in silence and wonder before the mystery of God, whose thoughts and ways are not even our most orthodox thoughts and ways. Their proper respect for the authority of scripture tends to become exaggerated confidence in their own ability to give the one right answer to all questions, solve all problems, resolve all ambiguities—even those that scripture itself leaves unanswered, unsolved, and unresolved. Their confidence in the infallibility of their biblical interpretation, theological speculation, and rational analysis and deduction leads them to accuse of heresy, falsehood, and error anyone within or outside the church who disagrees with them on any issue, historical and scientific as well as theological. They overestimate their own knowledge and underestimate that of everyone else. They know too much.

There are of course both religious and secular theories and practices that Christians should condemn. Christians do have the responsibility critically to evaluate all claims to truth in light of biblical revelation and theological reflection. But the exaggerated self-confidence of orthodox Christians often leads them to believe that their superior wisdom qualifies them to speak to others without listening, to instruct without needing instruction, to help without needing to be helped, to correct without themselves needing to be corrected. This self-confidence has led orthodox Christians to make some badly mistaken judgments on theological, ethical, scientific, and social issues. It has brought ridicule and contempt on the Christian movement as a whole. It has sometimes had disastrous consequences for the human community in general. But from the perspective of orthodoxy itself, perhaps the greatest danger of its self-confidence is that it is self-defeating. It contradicts at least four affirmations of orthodox theology itself and in so doing prevents orthodox Christians from realizing their own goal of understanding and defending authentic Christian faith and life in the church and in the public sphere.

The fallibility and sinfulness of all human beings. Orthodox theology teaches that all human beings are limited, fallible, and sinful. But orthodox Christians tend to forget that this applies to them too. They tend to forget that the wisdom of even the most orthodox Christians is shaped not only by biblical revelation and "objective" theological reflection but also by their own personal temperament and prejudices, by the self-interest of the economic class and political group to which they belong, and by the philosophical, cultural, and scientific presuppositions of the particular time and place in which they live. They may see how such factors distort the understanding of others, but they have difficulty seeing how these factors distort their own perception of the truth. In their blindness to their own fallibility and sinfulness they tend to close themselves to the possibility of self-correction and new insights that come from the very truth they seek to defend.

The work of the Holy Spirit in the church. Orthodox theology (especially in the Reformed tradition) emphasizes both the need and the promise of the "inward illumination" of the Holy Spirit to enable individual Christians and the Christian community to perceive the truth of God in scripture. But when orthodox Christians confront other Christians who disagree with them, they tend to forget their own theology of the Spirit. Too sure that it is always "them" and not possibly "us" who are mistaken, they often call into question their own confession that all Christians—including orthodox Christians—stand in constant need of the judging and correcting guidance of the Spirit. To the extent that they refuse to listen to what other Christians may have learned from the Spirit, they call into question not only the trustworthiness of their fellow Christians but also the trustworthiness of God's promise of the Spirit not just to a few Christians who are "like us" but to all Christians. When they are unwilling to recognize the possible guidance of the Spirit in and through other Christians, they call into question their own expressed desire to know and defend the truth that comes through the Spirit.

The work of the Spirit outside the church. Orthodox theology teaches that the Holy Spirit promised especially to Christians and the church is not bound to the little circle of believers in the world. The Spirit of God is like the wind that blows where it wills (John 3:8). The same life-giving, renewing, enlightening Spirit who brings truth, love, justice, beauty, joy, and peace to the hearts and minds of Christians can also work in the hearts and minds of other people. As John Calvin put it:

> If we regard the Spirit of God as the sole fountain of truth, we shall neither reject the truth itself, nor despise it wherever it shall appear, unless we wish to dishonor the Spirit of God. For by holding the gifts of the Spirit in slight esteem we contemn and reproach the Spirit himself. . . . If the Lord has willed that we be helped in [the arts and sciences] by the work and ministry of the ungodly, let us use this assistance. For if we neglect God's gift freely offered in these arts, we ought to suffer just punishment for our sloths.[5]

But orthodox Christians tend to forget their own doctrine of the Spirit when they look outside the Christian circle—especially when they confront truth claims of non-Christian religions and the modern natural and social sciences. Insofar as they are unable or unwilling to recognize the work of God's Spirit in the thought and lives of non-Christian and secular people, they "contemn and reproach the Spirit himself" and close themselves to the very truth they want to know and defend.

The authority of scripture. Orthodox Christianity (especially but not exclusively in the Protestant tradition) emphasizes the normative authority of biblical teaching in all theological discussion and debate. But, as we have noted, orthodox Christians tend in fact to make their particular interpretation and application of scripture to be their real final authority. As a result, their confession of the subservience of all theology to scripture tends to become fact insistence on the subservience of scripture to their particular theology: Biblical truth can be only what orthodox theology allows it to be. The classical Reformation doctrine of scripture should invite orthodox Christians to be "always reforming" as they continually learn new truth from the God who once spoke and continues to speak through scripture. But in fact their doctrine of scripture often becomes a barrier to reformation and the learning of new truth.

All four of the affirmations of classical orthodoxy we have mentioned point to the same conclusion: Orthodox Christians need to take their own orthodoxy more seriously. Precisely when they do that, they will also discover that they must incorporate into their view of Christian faith and life some insights from the other types of Christianity. To these we now turn, as we seek an understanding of what it means to be a Christian that is not *less* but *more* orthodox than that of Christians whose theme song is "Faith of Our Fathers."

2

They'll Know We Are Christians by Our Love

And they'll know we are Christians
by our love, by our love;
Yes, they'll know we are Christians
by our love.[1]

In the last chapter we discussed the orthodox understanding of what it means to be a Christian. In this and the following chapter we will discuss two forms of what in our time is called theological "liberalism." Like the orthodox understanding of Christian faith and life, both forms have their roots in the Bible itself and to some extent have always been present in the church. But the movement we call liberalism is the more immediate consequence of theological developments during the past two centuries. The word "liberal" comes from the Latin *liber,* "free." Modern theological liberalism is the result of the quest of some Christians in the eighteenth and nineteenth centuries to be free. They wanted freedom *from* the abstract theological speculation, supernaturalism, otherworldliness, authoritarianism, intolerance, and bitter conflict that were characteristic of both Catholic and Protestant churches in the seventeenth century, "the age of orthodoxy." And they wanted freedom *for* the discovery of an understanding of Christian faith and life that was open to learn from and contribute to the modern scientific, political, economic, cultural, and social developments they believed would improve the moral and spiritual quality of personal and collective life in the world. Moreover, they set about this task with optimistic confidence in their own moral potential and in that of human nature in general.

What is a Christian? Not so much a person who *believes* certain things but a person who *lives* a certain way. Christians are recognized not by what they think but by what they do, not by a list of doctrines they accept but by their way of life. Christianity is a matter of deed, not creed, something practical, not theoretical. Nor is it enough to devote oneself to pious exercises such as reading the Bible, praying, going to church, and turning to God to be blessed and saved. It is a matter of committed, hardworking service for God and neighbor in every area of everyday life. In short, true Christianity is a kind of higher and better *morality*.

This moral understanding of what it means to be a Christian has taken many quite different forms in the history of the church.

It may take the legalistic form of emphasis on strict obedience to the moral law of God as it is known in scripture (the Ten Commandments, for instance) and perhaps in the created order of the world.

It may take the more radical form of commitment to following the example of Jesus, emphasizing sexual purity, nonviolence, and poverty or a life of simplicity and self-denial.

It may take the form of an emphasis on a particular understanding of "holiness," identifying Christian life with the rejection of such "worldly" pursuits as drinking, dancing, smoking, gambling, theatergoing, and violation of the Sabbath.

Beginning with the Enlightenment in the eighteenth century, it has often taken a bourgeois form that has become very widespread in American civil religion. Christian morality is a kind of lowest-common-denominator morality that is believed to be characteristic of all people with "moral integrity" or "high ideals" or "ethical principles and values," whatever their religious affiliation or lack of it. This results in a sort of Boy Scout Christianity: Christians are simply people who are trustworthy, loyal, helpful, friendly, courteous, kind, cheerful, brave, clean, and reverent.

The most recent popular form of morally defined Christianity can be identified by the hymn I have chosen to summarize perhaps the highest and best form of this type of Christianity. A Christian is a person who is generous, compassionate—*loving*—in all relationships with other people. "They'll know we are Christians by our love."

All these quite different views of what it means to be a Christian have in common their emphasis on the moral rather than on the intellectual or merely "spiritual" aspect of Christian faith and life: A Christian is understood in one way or another to be a "good" person. In this chapter we will concentrate on what we have identified as the most recent version of this understanding of what it means to be a Christian, but what we say is applicable also to the other versions.

In Defense of Liberal Moralism

At least three strong arguments can be made in defense of Christianity understood in moral terms.

Biblical Support

A wealth of biblical material could be cited in support of this type of Christianity; we will mention only a few examples. Although Jesus was critical of pharisaical legalism, he said that he came not to abolish but to fulfill the law of God, and he demanded an even stricter obedience to the law than that of the Pharisees—obedience to the *law of love,* which he said (like Paul after him) is the summary of all the commandments of God. Jesus said that it is not those who piously say "Lord, Lord" (similar to "Praise the Lord") but those who *do the will of God* who will enter the kingdom of God. He said that whether we go to heaven or hell depends on whether we feed the hungry, clothe the naked, care for strangers, and minister to prisoners—not on whether we believe in the infallibility of scripture or the virgin birth or the substitutionary atonement. He invited those who are sinful and heavy-laden to come to him for comfort and help, but he made it clear that to live in his company is not just to receive the blessings and salvation he promises but to live a life of nonviolent love (even in dealing with our enemies) and to put service of the kingdom of God even above family responsibilities, financial security, and our own personal happiness. The Christianity Jesus proclaimed and demonstrated in his own life is more than orthodox belief, religious ritual, and pious receptivity. It is a kind of higher morality, a morality that goes beyond mere conventional respectability and legalistic conformity to what the law requires. It is the morality of love. If the teaching and example of Jesus is a clue to what it means to be a Christian, Christians should indeed be able to sing, "They'll know we are Christians by our love."

Support from the Protestant Reformation

Second, in defense of this "liberal" type of Christianity, we may mention the theology of John Calvin, whose orthodoxy is above reproach and who through the Puritan movement had a very strong influence on all traditional American Christianity.

Calvin knew something about what it means to defend orthodox faith, but when he came in the third book of his *Institutes of the Christian Religion* to talk about what it means to be a Christian[2] he did not discuss a list of essential doctrines or confessional formulas. He knew more than he is often given credit for about personal spirituality and what we call spiritual development, but for him that was not the heart of the matter either. When Calvin talked about what it means to be a Christian he talked especially about *sanctification,* continually changing and growing toward a new life lived in grateful and obedient response to God's "benevolence" toward us. And he summarized that life by talking about self-denial and cross-bearing shaped by "meditation on the future life." Calvin could hardly have written a cheerful little ditty called "They'll Know We Are Christians by Our Love," but when we look behind his gloomy chapter titles to the content of the chapters, we see that he too knew that the heart of Christian faith and life is a moral life of disciplined and free love for God and neighbor.[3]

The Calvinistic understanding of what it means to be a Christian has sometimes degenerated into a humorless, compulsive legalism. Its emphasis on God's transforming and demanding sanctifying grace has sometimes led Calvin's followers to neglect (as Calvin himself did not) the good news of God's accepting, forgiving, justifying grace. But even at its worst it has always been a strong necessary protest against a lazy, passive, self-centered Christianity that peddles what Dietrich Bonhoeffer later called "cheap grace," a Christianity that wants the gifts and blessings of God without the costly discipleship that goes with being a Christian.[4] If emphasis on disciplined, active service of God and neighbor is "liberal" Christianity, then we have to count Calvin and his followers among the founders of liberalism.

Practical Support

Finally, we may mention a practical argument in favor of Christianity understood as a kind of higher morality. We are more likely to be successful in our evangelistic efforts to recruit new Christians if we demonstrate the meaning of Christian faith and life in our own lives. We are more likely to win others to Christ by demonstrating Christlike love than by threatening them with what will happen to them if they do not accept the right ideas about Christ—or by bribing them with what will happen to them if they do. We are more likely to interest skeptics in investigating the truth of the Christian faith by the quality of the lives it produces than by theological arguments about the existence of God, the deity of Christ, or the authority of scripture. We are more likely to make Christian faith and life attractive to all the lost, aimless, bored people (especially young people) so typical of our time by showing them a cause worth giving themselves to than by trying to rival in a spiritual way all the ways our consumer society provides for them to care for their own health, wealth, happiness, and success. We are more likely to win public support for Christian ethical standards by the way Christians themselves live by them than by trying to get laws passed to force everyone to live like Christians. If they cannot know we are Christians by our love—by our Christian moral behavior—how else can they know what it means to be a Christian and want to become Christians themselves?

Criticism of Liberal Moralism

Nevertheless, there are some serious criticisms to be made of Christianity understood in moral terms, even in terms of the highest morality of love.

The Uniqueness of Christian Faith and Life

There can be no doubt that whatever else Christianity is, it includes morality in the deepest and highest sense of the word. But when we talk about Christian faith and life in these terms, have we got to the heart of what it means to be a Christian? After all, other people can be loving, compassionate, moral people too. In fact there are people who confess other religious faiths or no religious faith at all who put us Christians to shame by their moral integrity and by their willingness to sacrifice their own comfort, security, and self-interest for the welfare of other people. Anyone who has ever tried to argue with people that they should go to church and become Christians because they will be "better people" for it, or because Christians are morally superior, knows that the argument is lost every time. The targets of such arguments can always point to a Jew or an agnostic they know who never darkens the door of a church but is far more honest, caring, and self-giving than "those hypocrites" in the churches. It is true what they say: You *can* be "just as good" without going to church and becoming a Christian. What is distinctive of Christian faith and life cannot be less, but it must be more than what can be described in even the highest and best moral categories.

Consequences for Christian Self-understanding

A second weakness of morally defined Christianity is revealed in what it does to Christians' understanding of themselves. Christians whose theme song is some variation of "They'll Know We Are Christians by Our Love" are bound to ask themselves, "Am I good enough to call myself a Christian? Have I done enough? Have I really loved *all* my neighbors with *all* my heart, soul, mind, and strength? Will they really know that I am a Christian when they see how great is my moral integrity, my ethical purity, my love and compassion?" Then, if such Christians are serious about their Christian commitment, they work harder and harder to become really good, really loving, really Christian. And finally one of two things happens. Either they give up in despairing anxiety and guilt, convinced that they are not and never will be qualified to call themselves Christians. Or they convince themselves that they have made it: They really are law-abiding, loving, compassionate, truly Christian people. And they fall into smug self-congratulation, proud of their superiority to all those other people who are less moral, less loving, less Christian than they.

People who sing "They'll Know We Are Christians by Our Love" with cheerful ease and self-confidence are probably worse off than those who sing it with nagging guilty consciences. For who is more insufferable and less Christian than people who know and talk about how "good" and "loving" or "Christlike" they are? But in either case, whether it leads to self-hatred or to self-congratulation, morally defined Christianity has self-defeating consequences.

Consequences for Relationship with God and Other People

All Christians know, of course, that loving and serving God and our neighbors is what Christian life is all about. But when our theme song becomes some version of "they'll know we are Christians by how good and loving we are," Christian faith and life subtly become *Christian*-centered and *self*-oriented rather than *God*-centered and *neighbor*-oriented. The spotlight comes to shine very brightly on us, while God and neighbor recede into the background. Indeed, instead of loving and serving them for themselves, we tend to use them for the achievement of our own moral purity and the prestige and satisfaction it gives us. We begin serving God not because of our thanksgiving for God's goodness to us and not because we want to advance God's cause in the world but because it makes *us* happy, gives *us* inner peace, makes us "feel good" about *ourselves.* We begin loving and helping other people not for their own sakes but as objects for us to practice our goodness and kindness on, or because it makes us feel worthwhile and important when we see how much others need us, depend on us, appreciate and admire us. We begin explaining why we serve God and other people by saying, "It's the only way *I* can be happy, find meaning in *my* life, fulfill *myself.*"

When it is no longer God and neighbor but our own moral purity or Christlikeness that stands at the center of our Christian faith and life, we Christians are in danger of becoming just as self-serving as the most self-centered non-Christians who seek to build themselves up and find self-esteem and self-fulfillment in less pious ways.

Christianity Without Grace

The fundamental fault behind all other faults of Christianity defined in terms of the potential or actual moral achievements of Christians is that it tends to be Christianity without God's grace and therefore without awareness of the depths of human sin.

Do-it-yourself Christianity. Christians who define their Christian faith and life in terms of their own morality are well-meaning, serious Christians. They want to obey the commandments of God. They want to love God and other people with their whole being. They want to be Christlike. But they tend to forget (or they never learned or do not want to learn) the good news of the New Testament that the moral purity, compassion, and love they seek are the free gift of God's grace, not the result of their own efforts to prove and improve themselves. They tend to think that they must and can be self-motivated, self-sufficient, "mature" people who "take moral responsibility for themselves" in their moral struggles.

Such Christians believe in God, of course, but their God (similar to the God of orthodox Christianity) tends to be an absentee God, a God who once long ago in the laws of nature discernible in creation and in biblical revelation gave us the moral rules, principles, and ideals we need to live by, endowed us with the rational ability to interpret and apply them, built into us a conscience to remind us of them and the moral capacity to live by them—then left us on our own.[5]

Such Christians also believe in Christ. But for them Christ tends to be only a great teacher from the distant past who once long ago taught the "law of love," commanded us to live by it, and demonstrated it so perfectly himself that we are inspired to follow his example.

The New Testament gives us some justification for understanding Christianity as following the example of Jesus or as the "imitation of Christ." Jesus called his followers to a life like his of self-denial and cross-bearing (Mark 8:34), service (Mark 10:42–44), and love (John 15:12). First Peter 1:21 says that in his self-giving suffering Jesus "set an example" for us and that we should "follow in his steps." In 1 Corinthians 11:1 Paul tells the Corinthian Christians, "Be imitators of me, as I am of Christ," and in Philippians 2:1–7 he instructs the Philippian Christians to model their lives after Christ's self-humbling servanthood. But while such passages may help us to know in a general way how we should live as Christians, there are several reasons why an understanding of Christian faith and life based on following Jesus' example or imitating him is inadequate and even dangerous.

First, the New Testament does not tell us enough about Jesus' life for us to model our lives on his in detail. It does not intend to give us a full biography of Jesus, but only to give us the minimal biographical information necessary to tell us what he said and did as the proclaimer and bringer of the kingdom of God. Even if we did know more details of his life as a man who lived in the ancient Near East, that would not answer many of the most perplexing questions we have about how to live as faithful Christians in a modern industrial and technological society, not to mention questions that are uniquely related to the life of *women*. (What does it mean for a woman to live like the man Jesus?) We simply do not know enough about what Jesus did or would do in every situation to build a theology and ethic on his example. All attempts to do so beyond identifying a few general characteristics of Christian life involve too much guesswork to be trustworthy.

Second, most attempts to build a theology and ethic on the imitation of Jesus tend to be very selective. One Christian or group of Christians, for instance, may insist that all Christians should imitate his celibacy but not necessarily his nonviolence. Others opt for nonviolence but not celibacy. Some emphasize the example of his personal devotional life but ignore his prophetic ministry. Others neglect the example of Jesus' own personal piety and emphasize only his prophetic criticism of *false* piety and his political activism. Some argue that we are to follow his example only when he specifically commanded it, while others say that we are to do so even if he did not specifically command it. Different types of Christians tend to select, forget, or reject examples from Jesus' life to fit their own particular interests and concerns.

Third, it is by no means obvious that Christians *ought* to imitate all the details of Jesus' life, even if they could avoid such selectivity. Jesus was a particular person with a particular calling from God and a particular task to perform in a particular historical situation. Other people with different callings and different tasks in different situations may not be called to live exactly as he did, or even as he commanded his first disciples to live. A theology built only on commitment to follow Jesus' example or to imitate his way of life gives us very little help in deciding which aspects of his life should be imitated by all Christians in every time and situation, which should be imitated by only a few with a particular calling, and which relate only to his particular task. This question becomes especially perplexing when we move from such general activities as serving and loving to specific questions about whether Christians should be married, own property, defend their own and others' lives, and how they should relate their responsibility to serve the kingdom of God to their responsibility to care for their families.

Fourth, Christians cannot and should not try to imitate precisely those aspects of Jesus' life that are most important. We cannot and should not try to be what he was and do what he did as the one in whom God was uniquely present and at work. Jesus alone is the world's judge, savior, reconciler, and lord. It would be a terrible burden and unwarranted presumption for Christians to imitate Jesus by making themselves to be the judges, saviors, reconcilers, and lords of other people, forgetting that they too are judged by him, need to be reconciled and saved, and are called to live under his authority. Church history is full of examples of the disastrous consequences of well-meaning Christians acting as if *following* Jesus means to *replace* him, to claim for themselves the authority and saving power that belongs to him alone.

Fifth, Christians who understand themselves as the imitators of Christ tend to shift the emphasis from the one imitated to the imitators, calling attention to themselves rather than to him. They tend to imply that the truth of the Christian gospel and the validity of the Christian way of life stand or fall with who *they* are and what *they* do and say rather than with who *he* is and what *he* says and does. To imply that "we are Christians" means "we are like Jesus" or even "we *try* to be like Jesus" subtly puts Jesus himself in the shadows, Christians in the spotlight, and more often than not Christianity itself in a bad light.

Finally, a theology and ethic based on the example or on imitation of Jesus is based primarily on the four Gospels and tends to neglect what the rest of the New Testament tells us about the meaning of Christian faith and life. Those who seek to understand what it means to be a Christian from such a narrow base deprive themselves of what Acts and the epistles tell us about Christian faith and life in light of Jesus' resurrection and ascension, the enlightening and guiding presence of the Holy Spirit, the life and mission of the Christian community, and in general the shape of individual and corporate Christian life lived out between Jesus' earthly life and his coming again. We are not contemporaries of the earthly Jesus, as were the first disciples we hear about in the Gospels. Our situation is more like that of Christians in the rest of the New Testament, when the earthly Jesus was no longer with them. This does not mean that we should ignore or neglect the Gospels' understanding of Christians as followers of Jesus who are called to follow his example. It does mean that we need to pay attention also to the images, language, and concepts used in the rest of the New Testament to talk about what it means to be a Christian. Listening to the *whole* New Testament can help us correct the one-sidedness, answer at least some of the difficult questions, and avoid the dangers that result from an attempt to base our understanding of Christian faith and life exclusively on the example or the imitation of Jesus.

There tends to be little sense of need in moralistic Christianity (even when it is understood as following the example of Jesus) for the biblical promise of a present God and a risen and living Christ to accompany Christians on their way, creating in them a clean heart, giving them a new and right spirit, continually guiding them in their moral decisions, enabling them to do what they cannot do by themselves. Christians who set out to be the kind of people who can sing about how their Christianity is recognized in their own righteousness and love may be courageous and hardworking Christians, but they are in danger of wanting and thinking they can achieve Christianity without the grace of God—a Christianity without the very God they set out to serve.

The problem of sin. As Christians who feel no need for God's helping ("sanctifying") grace overestimate their own potential or actual virtue, so also they underestimate their own sinfulness and need for God's forgiving ("justifying") grace. They may be aware of the presence of sin in their lives, but their sense of their sinfulness is not so serious that it drives them to God for forgiveness and help; it only drives them to work harder to overcome their own sins and fulfill the requirements of God's law by themselves. They may convince themselves (at least for a while) that this is the right solution to the problem of sin. But they can do so only by interpreting the law of God in such a way that they hide the extent of their sin from themselves. They selectively reduce God's commandments to what is possible for them to obey, and they conveniently forget what they cannot and do not want to do (the Sermon on the Mount is often the first to go). They emphasize external sinful acts they do not do, and they ignore the sinful motives and desires in their hearts. Or they tell themselves that what really matters is not "mere" external obedience but whether one has good intentions and "means well." They justify failure to attain the perfect obedience God requires by telling themselves that they are at least more godly and Christlike than other people. The means of self-deception are inexhaustible.

There are those modern Pharisees, for instance, who assure themselves of their righteousness because they do not murder, steal (except maybe just a little at income-tax time), or commit adultery. But when it comes to what Jesus said about greed for more and more worldly goods and pleasures, or about the danger of accumulating money and possessions, they convince themselves that what Jesus called sin is really a great virtue, perhaps the greatest of all American virtues. They gladly sing "They'll Know We Are Christians by Our Love" when they think of their own families, others who are like them, and even some "worthy" and "deserving" people who are different. But their very God-fearing, law-abiding virtue excuses them from even trying to love criminals who commit capital offenses, anyone who is "pro abortion," communists, homosexuals, and all those "lazy worthless people" on the welfare rolls.

Even more accomplished in hiding their sinfulness from themselves, perhaps, are those who convince themselves of their moral superiority and Christlikeness by becoming what Karl Barth once called anti-Pharisee Pharisees. They pride themselves on their compassionate, understanding, and accepting attitude toward those who are guilty of even the most unacceptable personal and social sins and toward all those poor "outsiders" who are not "like us." It is all those self-righteous, pious legalists whom these Christians self-righteously and piously despise. They too can sing "They'll Know We Are Christians by Our Love," but their antimoralistic moralism prevents them from even trying to love those hard-hearted, uptight right-wing conservatives who are pro capital punishment and anti abortion, who are for the rich and against the poor, for forced conformity to their way of life and against freedom and tolerance.

Then there are those of us who are sure that *we* are the real Christians because we see what is wrong both with self-righteous right-wingers and with self-righteous left-wingers. We love both of them. We would like to help everyone become as open, compassionate, and generous as we are.

The point is that all of us are sinners, and therefore all of us try to manipulate God's law and Christ's teachings to justify ourselves and prove our moral superiority. But the more we try to overcome the sinfulness we see in others and prove ourselves superior to them, the deeper we are caught in the very sinfulness we want to overcome.

There are probably at least moments when even the most self-righteous people, on the right and on the left, know what Paul meant when he cried, "I can will what is right, but I cannot do it. For I do not do the good I want, but the evil I do not want is what I do. . . . Wretched person that I am! Who will deliver me from this body of death?" (Rom. 7:18–19, 24). But the tragedy of Christians who are committed to a do-it-yourself Christianity is that they cannot discover the deliverance Paul discovered: "Thanks be to God through Jesus Christ our Lord!" (Rom. 7:25). They are condemned either to give up the struggle in despairing self-contempt or to set out on an unending, self-defeating quest in this way or that to deliver themselves and make themselves into people who can point to *their own* righteousness and love. So long as they persist in this quest they are doomed to a Christianity that, no matter how well-meaning and serious it may be, is finally superficial and trivial because it understands neither the depths of human sin nor the depths of God's forgiving and renewing grace.

The Individualism of Morally Defined Christianity

A final weakness of morally defined Christianity is its tendency to limit the scope of Christian faith and life to personal morality and interpersonal relationships. Any understanding of what it means to be a Christian that is faithful to scripture must of course include concern for the moral integrity of individual Christians and the loving character of their personal relationships with other people. But according to scripture, true Christian faith and life involves more than that. It has to do also with the faith and life of the *community* of Christians who live together in thankful and obedient dependence on God's guiding, forgiving, and helping grace. Moreover, it has to do with the corporate responsibility of this community to participate in God's work to renew the structures and institutions of the world. Christianity defined in terms of personal morality and loving relationships does not necessarily exclude this corporate emphasis, but it could be—and often has been—interpreted to mean that insofar as the church is important at all, it is important only to the extent that it nourishes the faith and life of its individual members. It could be—and often has been—interpreted to emphasize the achievement of personal Christian relatedness and responsibility at the expense of commitment to social justice.

This criticism brings us to a second type of liberal Christianity, one that seeks to overcome the individualistic tendencies of Christianity defined in terms of personal morality and love. It is perhaps no accident that one of the most sexist hymns in our hymnbooks expresses this type of Christianity at its best—and worst.

3
Rise Up, O "Men" of God!

Rise up, O men of God!
  Have done with lesser things;
Give heart and soul and mind and strength
  To serve the King of kings.

Rise up, O men of God!
  His Kingdom tarries long;
Bring in the day of brotherhood
  And end the night of wrong.

What does it mean to be a Christian? It means for Christian men—and women—to have a vision of a better world in which there is justice, freedom, peace, and plenty for all. It means to have a vision of a new humanity in which every person is recognized as our brother (*or* sister). It means to have a vision of what the New Testament calls the coming of the kingdom of God. It is not enough to believe the right things. Nor is it enough to accept Christ as our personal Lord and Savior and to receive the blessings and "benefits" God promises in him. Nor is it yet enough just to get our personal lives and relationships in order. To be a Christian is to bring the sovereignty of God or the lordship of Christ to bear on the social and political life of the world. The gospel that shapes Christian faith and life is a "social gospel," and true Christians are those who believe that Christian love is neither real nor effective until it expresses itself as justice in the social order. Traditional Christian doctrine and traditional biblical interpretation are to be accepted, revised, reinterpreted, or rejected according to whether they encourage and enable Christians to accept their responsibility for creating a new world and a new humanity, the kingdom of God on earth, here and now.

This understanding of what it means to be a Christian is sometimes called "nineteenth-century liberalism," because in its modern form it was developed in the nineteenth and early twentieth centuries as an expansion and correction of the theology of the eighteenth-century Enlightenment we discussed in the last chapter. But its earliest roots lie in the Old and New Testaments, and in various forms it has always been present in the church. Even in its modern form it would be a mistake to identify any one view of how Christians are to "bring in" or "realize" the kingdom of God as *the* position of theological liberalism. Christianity understood as social activism can be expressed in a wide variety of social-political strategies, depending on what Christian individuals or groups believe the kingdom of God on earth looks like and how they believe it can be achieved.[1]

In the United States and other Western countries today most social-gospel Christians believe that a new and better world will come through gradual evolutionary reform accomplished by the democratic process and constitutional change.

Others, like the founders of the American republic two hundred years ago and like the advocates of Liberation Theology in Latin America today, believe that the forces of oppression and injustice are so strong that only violent revolution can overthrow them and inaugurate the rule of God's justice and peace on earth.

Still others, like Martin Luther King and his followers, believe that the goal can be achieved only by nonviolent resistance to unjust laws and systems and institutions.

More recently, some Christians (who would be highly offended to be called liberals) have tied the coming of the kingdom of God to the success of anticommunistic nationalism, superiority in the nuclear arms race, the success of the capitalistic economic system, and legislative and judicial enforcement of what they believe to be Christian morality and spirituality.

Though their methods may be quite contradictory, all these Christians have in common the conviction that to be a Christian means to work for the realization of the rule of God on earth here and now—and the conviction that in one way or another they can achieve this goal. Though they may not be able to do anything else together, and may mean something quite different when they do it, all these Christians can stand up and sing together, "Rise up, O men of God! . . . The kingdom tarries long. . . . Give heart and soul and mind and strength to serve the King of kings . . . And end the night of wrong."

Very careful attention needs to be given to the critical evaluation of the different goals and strategies in the minds of those who make this their theme song. But our task now is not to decide between them. It is to ask whether we ought to sing the hymn at all (even if we clean up its sexist language). To what extent is it correct to define what it means to be a Christian in terms of any attempt, whatever its political and social orientation, to bring in the kingdom of God through Christian social and political activity? Or, to put it in other words, what are the common strengths and weaknesses of any Christian whose theme song is some version of "Rise Up, O Men of God!"?

In Defense of Liberal Social Activism

Biblical Support

Social-gospel Christians—right, left, and middle-of-the-road—have the Bible on their side. To acknowledge and serve the God of the Bible is to acknowledge and serve the God who is creator and ruler of the whole world, including its social and political structures. The prophets never tire of saying that correct belief, personal piety, individual morality, and proper religious ritual are empty and hypocritical unless they are accompanied by social justice for the poor and oppressed of the earth. The Gospels agree that Jesus came proclaiming and bringing not just the salvation of individual souls, or an orthodox theological system, or a new and better personal morality, but the kingdom of God—a new order of reconciling love and justice for the sake of those who are spiritually, morally, physically, economically, or politically weak and oppressed. Jesus taught us to pray that God's kingdom may come and God's will be done on *earth*. The first Christians summarized everything they believed by confessing their allegiance to the risen Jesus who is Lord not just in the hearts of individual believers or in the church but over all the principalities, powers, and authorities of the earth, including those that rule in and through political and social institutions and structures. When they looked to the future, these first Christians did not look forward to escape from their humanity in this world to a purely spiritual existence in *another* world; they hoped and worked for the renewal of their humanity in a new creation of *this* world. From beginning to end the Bible proclaims a social-political gospel. From beginning to end it teaches that to believe in God or in Jesus or in the Holy Spirit is to "rise up" and serve God by doing justice and working for a social-political order that reflects the justice of the kingdom of God on earth.

Support from the Reformation

In support of this form of Christianity we may appeal especially to John Calvin. For Calvin and his followers, to believe in the sovereignty of God means to believe that God has a claim on every area of life, public as well as private, economic and political as well as religious. It is to believe, as H. Richard Niebuhr has put it, in a Christ who is the "Transformer" of culture, not in a Christ who sets us against culture, enables us to ignore and rise above it, or allows us to accept and bless whatever happens to be the social and political status quo.[2] To believe in the coming kingdom of Christ, as Calvin says in the famous last chapter of the *Institutes,* means to believe that Christians should recognize and support political leaders as God's representatives on earth, people who are called to "represent in themselves some image of divine providence, protection, goodness, benevolence and justice," to "preserve freedom and equity," to "help those forcibly oppressed," to "promote general peace and tranquillity," to defend the "lowly common folk" against tyrants—in short, to maintain "humanity among men." This high view of Christian political responsibility could even lead Calvin to say that "civil authority" (not the ordained Christian ministry!) is "the most sacred and by far the most honorable of all callings in the whole life of mortal men."[3]

This Christian "social humanism" led Calvin to set an example for his followers in succeeding generations by helping to establish in Geneva a social welfare system, public schools and hospitals, refugee centers to care for the victims of political and religious oppression, and the beginnings of a democratic form of government.[4] It also led future Calvinists to revolutionary protest against oppressive and tyrannical governments in France, Great Britain, the United States, and other countries around the world.[5]

Friendly as well as hostile critics have noted that there is another side to Calvinist social and political theology. With Calvin himself and those who followed him there has sometimes been a "theocratic" tendency to believe that the purpose of the state is not only to promote the common good of all people but to protect and enforce Christian (i.e., Calvinistic) morality, worship, and theology. Moreover, some Calvinist preachers, political leaders, and citizens have been too sure that their version of civil righteousness is the only correct version and have been too willing to impose it on everyone else. We will return to this danger presently. The point to be made now, however, is that Christians who believe that the Christian gospel is a social gospel and commit themselves to a just and humane social order can call on Calvin as well as on scripture to defend their understanding of Christian faith and life. If such an understanding of Christianity is political and social "liberalism" and "humanism," then Calvin is one of the founders of liberal humanism and his followers today can cheerfully confess that in their own way they are liberal humanists too.

Political and Theological Realism

A final argument in support of Christianity understood as working through political and social action to bring in the kingdom of God is that, especially in its various twentieth-century forms, this type of Christianity has insisted on a realistic (and biblical and orthodox) understanding of corporate human sinfulness and therefore of the need to use corporate power to solve the problem of human suffering and need. As Reinhold

Niebuhr[6] and, more recently, representatives of Liberation Theology[7] have pointed out, much human suffering is caused by unjust social, political, and economic systems and structures that serve the self-interest of some races, classes, cultural groups, and nations at the expense of others. But individuals and groups who control and benefit from these systems and structures never voluntarily give up their privileged position (partly because of their sinfulness and partly because, as Niebuhr said, none of us ever sees the needs of others as clearly as we see our own). They will accept radical social change necessary for the achievement of justice only when forced to do so by the use of some form of collective power. It may be the power of legislative or judicial reform, the power of economic boycott, or the power of a political party or movement that gains control by democratic or revolutionary means. But it is only by the collective use of power in one form or another that the victims of social structures and systems that exclude, oppress, and exploit them can be effectively helped or can effectively help themselves.

Christians who agree with this analysis of the situation face many difficult questions: What form of power, and how much, is necessary or permitted, likely to be effective or self-defeating in a particular situation? When, if ever, can Christians and the church support or cooperate with non-Christian or anti-Christian parties and movements that fight for social justice for the poor and oppressed? Given the fact that Christian churches themselves are often largely composed of the very people who control or benefit from unjust social and political systems and structures, how can we be faithful Christians and loyal members of the church at the same time?

But if we are truly committed to feed the hungry, clothe the naked, free the captive, and care for the homeless stranger, we cannot avoid facing the complexities and accepting the moral ambiguity of the use of power. It is not enough for us to do individual acts of compassion or to encourage the church and social welfare agencies to support programs of charity and philanthropy. Such an approach may salve our guilty consciences, but it too easily excuses us from working for the radical social, political, and economic changes that the poor and oppressed need most. It can in fact intensify social and political injustice by buying off the recipients of our benevolence and making them content with a survival existence of passive dependence instead of rising up to demand the opportunity to care for themselves. What the poor and oppressed need is justice, not our patronizing kindness and charity. If we are to go beyond the alleviation of symptoms to attack the basic causes of human need and suffering, what other alternative do we have than to seek realistic and appropriate forms of collective power that are necessary for the creation of a truly just society? How can either the rich and powerful or the poor and powerless know we are Christians unless they see that our love is expressed as the demand and fight for justice?

Criticism of Liberal Social Activism

Now we turn to the weaknesses of Christianity understood as commitment to a social gospel and the struggle for the social justice of the kingdom of God.

The Uniqueness of Christian Faith and Life

First we must ask the same question we asked about Christianity understood in moral categories: Have we identified what is really unique about Christians when we talk in these terms? Have we gotten to the heart of the biblical Christian understanding of Christian faith and life even when we move beyond thinking in terms of loving personal relationships to talk about just social relationships? After all, Christians are not the only people committed to social justice. Indeed, followers of other religious traditions and people who confess no religious faith at all often put Christians to shame by their willingness to sacrifice their own safety, security, reputation—even their own lives—for the sake of justice, freedom, and peace. We have only to look at the history of the struggle for racial justice in the United States or the opposition to Nazi tyranny in Germany or the fight for political and economic justice in Latin America today to see that all too often it is only after others have taken the risks, blazed the trail, paid the cost, and made it relatively safe and respectable that some Christians and churches have come along with a weak acquiescence or belated commitment to social justice. This is not to deny that there have been many Christians who have courageously worked as well as prayed for justice, freedom, and peace on earth. But even when we are most faithful in doing so, we cannot claim that this is what makes us unique as Christians. Being a Christian or a Christian church cannot mean less, but it must mean more than social and political activism.

God's Kingdom and Human Ideology

A second difficulty with Christianity understood as social action is that those committed to it so easily confuse it with some conservative, liberal, or revolutionary political or economic ideology. Activist Christians are tempted, for instance, to be sure that God is on the side of free enterprise capitalism and against Marxist or democratic socialism—or vice versa. They are tempted to identify the sovereignty of God with the military, economic, and political sovereignty of their nation—or to see God at work in every internal or external challenge of their nation's military, economic, and political policies. They are tempted to believe that the peace God wills can come only through groups that support nuclear disarmament—or nuclear deterrence. They are tempted to identify the will of God with whatever position they hold regarding abortion, capital punishment, prayer in schools, preferential treatment as a means to achieve justice for women and ethnic minorities, pornography, environmental protection, homosexuality, social programs to provide for the poor, and almost any other moral and social issue.

If Christians are to be faithful and effective servants of God in the world, they must certainly take sides on such critical issues and support the side they believe to be most consistent with the will of God for human welfare. But the unqualified identification of Christianity with this or that political, economic, or social position nearly always results in a serious ideological distortion of Christian faith and life.

There are at least three sure signs that indicate when such a distortion has happened, each of which is also an indication of the frequency with which it actually does happen.

1. In the first place, individual Christians and groups of Christians have confused commitment to the Christian gospel with commitment to an ideology when they assume that their particular liberal, conservative, or revolutionary political or economic program is the only possible one for true Christians. Christians are not free, of course, to pursue any political and economic goals and strategies they happen to like. But only in rare and extremely critical situations is there only one right way to work for justice, freedom, and peace. Moreover, even when we believe it necessary to criticize other Christians for being dangerously misguided or blind or unchristian at some point, that does not mean (again, except in extreme circumstances) that we can deny that they may be deeply committed Christians in other respects. It is a sure sign that Christian faith has been confused with some political, economic, or social ideology when a Christian too quickly, too often, says to another Christian or group of Christians, "Either you agree with me and do it my way or you are not a Christian at all."

2. Second, Christians have turned the gospel into an ideology when their ultimate concern is no longer to serve God and other human beings but some *cause.* When we listen only to those parts of the Bible that support our conservative, liberal, or revolutionary political or economic cause and ignore or try to explain away parts of scripture that point in a different direction—then we are committed to an ideology rather than to the Word of God. When we make or break friendships on the basis of people's usefulness to or cooperation with the political program and economic system we support—then we have sold out not only friendship

but the gospel itself to an ideology. The same is true above all when we sacrifice the *lives* of other people for the sake of a cause. There are indeed times when obedience to God requires us to hurt in order to heal, even to sacrifice life in order to save life. But when Christians justify an action or policy that hurts or destroys any human being or group of human beings by speaking too quickly and easily of the "painful" and "unfortunate" but "necessary" consequences of having to make "complex ethical decisions"—then we may be sure that we are dealing with commitment to an ideology and not to the Christian faith. For Christians, causes must serve people, not people, causes.[8] It is a sure sign that ideology has triumphed over Christian faith whenever the success of any cause, however good or Christian in itself, becomes more important than the value and dignity of human life that God in Jesus Christ wills for all people —including those who are enemies of the causes we support, for "they" are loved by God just as much as "we" are.

3. Finally, it is a sure sign that Christian faith has been confused with an ideology when Christians can only echo the one-sided, partial truths of this or that conservative, liberal, or revolutionary political or economic position, with no unique contribution to make from a specifically Christian perspective. This happens, for instance, when Christians can propose no alternative to Marxist collectivism other than capitalist individualism—or vice versa. Or when they can oppose repressive authoritarianism that robs people of personal freedom only by supporting permissive anarchy that encourages them to abdicate their responsibility for the common good—or vice versa. Or when they can combat false materialism only by advocating an equally false spirituality—or vice versa. Or when they know how to defend the cause of powerless outsiders only by expressing contempt for powerful insiders—or vice versa. *Or* when on such critical issues they invariably take a safely moderate "both-and" position that recognizes the problem but offers no concrete solutions other than some vague, general "balance" between opposing points of view. When Christians enter the struggle for justice, freedom, and peace knowing only how to parrot positions already taken by others, they deprive the human community of any specifically Christian contribution to social order. And they make the word "Christian" simply a synonym for this or that left-wing, right-wing, or middle-of-the-road ideology.

Nothing we have said means that Christians can take a neutral stance above all ideological parties and movements, criticizing all of them from a superior vantage point, refusing to have anything to do with any of them because each one is imperfect. Christians who are committed to the justice, freedom, and peace of the kingdom of God will inevitably find themselves drawn toward causes and movements that seem to them most

responsive to human need. Because of differences in their personal experience and temperament, and because of differences in the historical,
political, and sociological context in which they live, some Christians
will support conservative causes and movements, others liberal or revolutionary ones. But Christians committed to the kingdom of God can
never be counted on automatically to follow any party line on economic,
political, or social issues. They may be social-political liberals but they
can never be "knee-jerk" liberals. They may be social-political conservatives or revolutionaries, but they can never be absolutely predictable
conservatives or revolutionaries. They will always be at best the loyal
opposition in any party or movement, people who can never be trusted
to be unwavering true believers and who are therefore always a little
suspect among the party faithful. They will ask questions and express
reservations that make them seem too conservative to their fellow liberals or revolutionaries, too liberal or revolutionary to their fellow conservatives. For Christians have a higher loyalty than their loyalty to *any*
party—loyalty to a Lord who judges, corrects, and rules over *all* parties.
Moreover, Christians will always disturb the party faithful by their
willingness to talk to, even learn from, other Christians who acknowledge the same Lord even though they belong to an opposition party. This
may be an uncomfortable position to be in, but if Christians do not
maintain relative independence in their political, economic, and social
commitments, how can they live as Christians, people who finally serve
neither this nor that ideology but the kingdom of God that comes not
just for the sake of liberals, conservatives, or revolutionaries but for the
sake of all?

It is especially difficult for Christians who identify Christianity with
struggle for a new social order to maintain this distinction between
commitment to the kingdom of God and commitment to an ideology.
One reason is that whether they are Republicans or Democrats, Marxists
or members of the Moral Majority, they all tend to have at least one false
presupposition in common. This brings us to our final criticism of Christians whose theme song is "Rise Up, O Men of God!"

God's Reign or Christians' Reign?

The common assumption of social-gospel Christians of all stripes tends
to be the belief that the coming of the kingdom depends on them and
that (with the help of God, of course) they are adequate to the task: The
righteousness, justice, peace, and freedom of God's rule will come as we
Christians successfully preserve and expand—or overthrow and replace
—this or that economic system or political regime. Or as we defeat this
or that enemy. Or as we establish—or abolish—this or that legislative or

judicial policy. Or as we increase—or reduce—the military power of this or that nation or coalition of nations. In one way or another the kingdom of God will come as *we* "bring it in," or "realize it," or perhaps "expand" it.

This confidence that the coming of the kingdom depends on Christians is wrong for two reasons.

1. In the first place, those who share this confidence underestimate the power of personal and corporate sin in the world. As a result, one of two things happens.

We commit ourselves as Christian individuals or as a Christian community to a liberal or conservative or revolutionary social or political cause that we are convinced is necessary and right. We work hard for it, pray passionately, go to meetings and rallies, serve on committees, form task forces, lobby for votes, join parties of like-minded persons, participate in protest marches, perhaps even sacrifice our own and our family's comfort and security. We stick it out through disappointments, setbacks, and defeats, against the opposition and indifference we meet on all sides. But the coming kingdom does not even draw near. And finally —all of a sudden or very gradually—we give up. Even if we continue to go through the motions, our heart is no longer in it. We have become weary in well-doing, burned out, and we drop out. Because we have assumed that the coming of the kingdom depends on the success of our plans, efforts, and schedules, we conclude that it will not and cannot come at all.

Or something that may be even worse happens: We are successful! The conservative, liberal, or revolutionary movement we support is victorious. The enemy is defeated. Our party gains control of the government. Bad laws are abolished and good laws are passed. Peace is achieved through an ever-expanding arms race or by total nuclear disarmament. In one way or another we get what we wanted. But sin and injustice only crop up in new forms that are just as destructive as the old forms. Changed laws have not changed people. Those who were the powerless and oppressed become powerful oppressors themselves. Law and order has been achieved, but only at the expense of justice and freedom; or freedom and legal rights have been achieved for some, but at the expense of justice for all. With or without nuclear weapons, nations are still threatened by wars and rumors of war. Things may be better than they were for a while, but evil is just as powerful as it was, and the kingdom of God seems just as far away as ever.

In other words, success as well as failure in our efforts to achieve the coming of the kingdom finally leads to disappointment and despair. In either case the tragic result is that the very people who care most and work hardest often give up the struggle and abandon the world to the very powers of sin and injustice and death they set out to challenge and overthrow.

2. But the tendency to believe that the coming of the kingdom of God on earth depends on us Christians or on our church is wrong not only because it underestimates the power of evil; it is above all wrong because it underestimates the power of God.

The Christian gospel is not the promise that if Christians work at it hard enough and long enough (not to mention collect enough money) *they* can overcome the power of evil and inaugurate the rule of God in the world. It is the promise that *God* will bring in God's own kingdom, with or without the sponsorship and cooperation of Christians.

The gospel does not give Christians the right or the responsibility to be the judges, saviors, reconcilers, rulers, and renewers of the world. It says that the job of Judge, Savior, Reconciler, Ruler, and Renewer has already been filled.

The gospel is not the bad news that Christ will be Lord if and when we convince enough individuals to "let" him be Lord or "make" him Lord of their lives, or if and when we collect enough votes, convert enough people, or start enough revolutions to *enable* him to be Lord over the world's political and economic structures. It is the good news that *God* has made him Lord and that God's victory over the powers of darkness, suffering, injustice, and death is already on the way and will surely come.

The gospel is about the kingdom of God, not about the kingdom of Christians.

Once again, this gospel does not mean that we are excused from living and working in anticipation of the new world and the new humanity that are on the way. Nor does it mean that God will not use our inadequate, blundering efforts. It does mean that we are delivered from the blasphemous belief that it can happen only as we make it happen. And it means that we do not have to fall into despair when it does not happen according to our plans and schedules. We can have the energy and confidence to keep up the struggle despite our failures—and despite our questionable successes—just because our hope is not in ourselves but in God.

> Hope in God gives us courage for the struggle. The people of God have often misused God's promises as excuses for doing nothing about present evils. But in Christ the new world has already broken in and the old can no longer be tolerated.
>
> We know our efforts cannot bring in God's kingdom. But hope plunges us into the struggle for victories over evil that are possible now in the world, the church, and our individual lives. Hope gives us courage and energy to contend against all opposition, however invincible it may seem, for the new world and the new humanity that are surely coming.[9]

The Christian gospel *is* a social gospel. Christians *are* people who by definition are committed to social justice and a new social order. To be a Christian includes not only praying but working that God's will may be done and God's kingdom come on earth. But a genuinely Christian hope for that kingdom is a different and far better one than hope for what liberal or conservative or revolutionary Christians can accomplish.

4
Amazing Grace

Amazing grace! how sweet the sound
That saved a wretch like me!
I once was lost, but now am found,
Was blind, but now I see.

The Lord has promised good to me,
His word my hope secures;
He will my shield and portion be
As long as life endures.

What does it mean to be a Christian? Not just to think the right things about God or Jesus, as the orthodox believe. Not just to be good or work for justice and peace, as theological liberals believe. Christian faith and life may include true belief, personal morality, and a social conscience, but people are not truly Christians until the source, the foundation and motivating power of all other characteristics of their faith and life, is a personal experience of the amazing grace of God. The fundamental thing that distinguishes Christians from other religious and moral people is that they are people who have been confronted with the good news of the grace of God in Jesus Christ for lost sinners, confessed that they are such sinners, repented of their sins, acknowledged Jesus Christ as their personal Lord and Savior, and consequently been converted and born again to live in dependence on his forgiveness, help, and protection. In short, Christians are people who have been "saved" and who enjoy the benefits of their salvation.

In the history of Protestant Christianity, this emphasis on the personal experience of salvation has been characteristic of a theological movement called "pietism," one of the most influential alternatives to the orthodox and liberal movements we studied in the preceding chapters. It is represented in the United States today by those Christians who believe that what is wrong with the church is that it has become so preoccupied with theoretical theological questions and social issues that it has forgotten that its main business is to confront people with their need to repent, make a personal decision for Christ, and claim the promises of God for their present and future salvation. The popularity of this understanding of what it means to be a Christian is confirmed by the fact that "Amazing Grace" is the favorite hymn of many Christians of all denominations. When we come now to evaluate the pietist view of Christian faith and life, therefore, we come not just to one of several possible views, but to the one that for many, perhaps most, Christians in our country is the heart of the matter.

In Defense of Christian Pietism

Following the pattern we have set in speaking of other types of Christianity, we will first say a good word for pietism and pietistic Christians.

Pietism and the Bible

In the first place, we can say that, like the other types of Christianity we have discussed, pietism too has a solid biblical foundation. One has only to look at the hundreds of biblical references to the words "salvation," "save," or "savior" to realize that this is a very important theme throughout scripture. Nor can we be faithful to the biblical message if we follow a popular trend today that shifts the emphasis from the personal to the corporate and speaks only of political and social "liberation" instead of personal salvation. We have not heard the whole Old Testament message if we hear only about the covenant promises God addressed to Israel as a whole and do not hear especially what Psalms, the prayer and hymnbook of Israel, tells us about the personal needs and problems, suffering and guilt, fears and hopes of individual believers and about the personal forgiveness, renewal, protection, and blessing they are promised. We have not heard the whole New Testament message if we hear only about the promised coming of God's kingdom of justice and peace and do not hear also the urgent invitation and command for individuals to repent, believe, make a personal commitment to Jesus Christ, and be born again—with the promise of blessing and salvation to those who respond to this invitation and the warning of judgment and condemnation to those who do not. We may be offended or made uncomfortable by this pietistic strain in both the Old and New Testaments, but it is undeniably there.

Pietism and Christian Tradition

A second argument in favor of the pietistic emphasis on personal salvation is that it is not only biblical but a main theme of classical Christian tradition. Pietism as such became a distinct and self-conscious movement through the initial influence of some late-seventeenth-century German

Lutheran theologians and pastors. It became a powerful influence on all American churches through the influence of the Presbyterian Jonathan Edwards, the Methodist John Wesley, and other preachers who in the eighteenth and nineteenth centuries were responsible for the revivalist movement that continues even in our time. But the pietistic emphasis on the experience of God's grace and its benefits did not begin only in the seventeenth century. After all, Luther had already identified the heart of the gospel as the experience of justification through faith alone. And when Calvin came in the third book of the *Institutes* to talk about what it means to be a Christian, he gave it the title "The Way in Which We Receive the Grace of Christ: What Benefits Come to Us from It, and What Effects Follow." Though the Reformers differed from the Roman Catholic tradition in their understanding of how salvation is achieved, they followed the early and medieval church in making salvation itself a main theme of Christian theology. When we come later to criticize pietistic preoccupation with "me and my salvation," we must be aware that what we are criticizing is not just one movement within Christian tradition but almost two thousand years of Christian tradition itself.

Pietism and Orthodoxy

A third argument in favor of pietism is that it represents a corrective for some of the one-sided tendencies of the orthodox understanding of Christian faith and life. Whereas orthodoxy can become a cold, rationalistic "head" religion, pietism is a warm religion of the "heart," based on feeling rather than thinking, on subjective personal experience rather than objective external authority.

Ask orthodox Christians what they believe, and they will tell you "what the Bible says" or "what the church teaches." Ask pietist Christians what they believe, and they will tell you first of all not about someone else's faith but about their own.

Ask orthodox Christians what it means to be a Christian, and they will define the doctrinal content of the Christian faith. Ask pietist Christians, and they will talk about their own personal relationship with the Lord.

Ask orthodox Christians for their personal testimony about the presence and work of God in their lives, and they often do not know what to say. Ask pietist Christians, and they are able and eager to answer in great detail.

Ask orthodox Christians about the meaning of salvation, and they will tell you about what God did for us two thousand years ago in the birth, death, and resurrection of Jesus Christ. Ask pietist Christians, and they will tell you "what Christ did for *me* at the hour I first believed." For a pietist Christian, Christ is not really born until he is born in *my* heart;

his death has no meaning until *my* old self has been put to death; he is not truly risen until he lives in *me*. Salvation has not happened until *I* repent, believe, and turn *my* life over to the Lord.

Orthodox Christianity tends to be clergy-dominated and church-centered, dependent on theologians and preachers who are the "experts" trained to understand and explain biblical and theological truth. Pietistic Christianity tends to be a religion of the laity, based not on what scholars or church authorities say but on their own private devotional reading of scripture, meditation on their own spiritual pilgrimage, and personal prayer life.

Pietistic Christianity can be criticized for being too emotional, too anti-intellectual, too individualistic, and too subjective (characteristics that make it especially appealing—and dangerous—in the United States, where the culture in general tends to be suspicious of the intellect and rebellious against any external authority or community obligation that limits the freedom and right of individuals to think and live as they please). But orthodox Christians need to be reminded that to love God is to love God with all our heart and soul as well as with all our mind. They need to be reminded that even the most profound and true thoughts about God are no substitute for a "personal walk" with God. They need to be warned about the complacency and hypocrisy that result from believing that anyone can be a Christian without personally experiencing and living by the reconciling and renewing grace of God. They need to be reminded that it is not primarily theologians and preachers but lay people who constitute the church of Jesus Christ and that scholarly study of scripture and public worship led by the minister are no substitute for personal Bible study and private devotional life.

Orthodox Christians, in other words, need to learn to experience and talk about the amazing grace of God that saved *me*, taught *my* heart to fear, relieved *my* fears, leads *me*, promises good to *me*, secures *my* hope, guards and protects *me*.

Pietism and Theological Liberalism

A fourth argument in favor of pietist Christianity has to do with the alternative it represents to moralistic or idealistic liberalism. Like liberals, some pietists tend to have a good deal of confidence in their own virtue and what it can accomplish, though pietists tend to concentrate on such virtues as sexual purity and abstinence from the use of alcohol rather than on such virtues as general moral integrity and political and economic justice. But the kind of pietism represented by the hymn "Amazing Grace," the kind that probably is the most popular in our time, is completely free of such self-confidence. Not a single line in

"Amazing Grace" speaks about what *Christians* must say and do and accomplish; the hymn speaks only about what *God* has done, is doing, and promises to do. This is the strength as well as the weakness of such pietism.

Liberals, when they are seriously committed Christians, are *busy* Christians. They work without ceasing to improve themselves, improve other people, improve the world around them. But their very moral seriousness often has unfortunate consequences. Because there are so many wrongs to be corrected, so much suffering to be relieved, so much injustice to be overcome, they tend to become driven, compulsive people who can never rest (much less play) without a guilty conscience. Moreover, as we have seen, they are prone to assume that what they cannot achieve will not and cannot be achieved at all. Their faith tends subtly to become faith not in God's wisdom, power, righteousness, and love but in their own.

Pietists whose theme song is "Amazing Grace," on the other hand, know what it means patiently to "wait on the Lord." They too want to serve God, but they know that when they have done the best they can, they can "turn it over to the Lord" and let the Lord "bear the burden" of their own and the world's needs and cares. They are free from the guilt, self-condemnation, and anxiety that comes from thinking that they have to be the saviors of the world. Their faith, hope, and confidence is not in themselves and the good they may be able to accomplish but in God and the good God promises and will certainly accomplish.

Expressed in technical theological language, pietists remember better than many liberals that Christians are not "justified" by their good works or by their hard work but by the free grace that accepts them despite the fact that they are unworthy sinners and inadequate servants. They remember better than many liberals that the salvation of individuals and of the world is not the task of Christians but the task of God. This leads us to a fifth argument in favor of pietist Christianity.

Pietist Experience of Joy and Peace

Both orthodox and liberal Christians tend to be so serious, so humorless. The truth has to be constantly defended against the ever-present danger of falsehood and heresy. There must be a never-ending war against sin, injustice, suffering, and death. But the lives of those who live by "amazing grace" are filled with the joy, peace, confidence, and assurance of salvation that comes from knowing how to "let go and let God." Pietist Christians sometimes achieve their happiness by ignoring or repressing awareness of the pain, brokenness, and injustice present in their own lives and in the world around them. Their cheerful piety can become trivial, unrealistic, insensitive, and a little too sweet. But at their best, they honestly acknowledge the "dangers, toils, and snares" in their own and others' lives, yet nevertheless experience the lighthearted freedom from anxiety that comes not from Pollyanna escapism but from the discovery of the amazing grace of God that penetrates even to the depths of their own and the world's guilt, need, and suffering. Pietists understand better than many liberal and orthodox Christians what Jesus was talking about when he said, "My peace I give to you. . . . Let not your hearts be troubled, neither let them be afraid" (John 14:27).

Pietism and the Holy Spirit

Finally in defense of the pietist movement, we may mention the serious attention it gives to the work of the Holy Spirit. The Spirit is not mentioned in the hymn we have chosen to represent this type of Christianity, but when those who have a personal experience of the amazing grace of God and its benefits are asked how they came to have such a great experience, their answer typically is "by the power of the Holy Spirit."

It is no accident that pietist Christians turn to the Holy Spirit to talk about their religious experience. The Spirit is the present work of God, making real in the lives of people here and now the saving, renewing, liberating work of Christ that took place on the first Good Friday and Easter Sunday two thousand years ago. God the Father is God the creator and ruler *over* us. God the Son is God the savior and reconciler *with* and *for* us. But the Holy Spirit is God the giver and renewer of life *within* us. The work of God the Father and God the Son is the "objective" work of God for all people everywhere, even before they know about it and experience it. But the work of God the Holy Spirit is the "subjective" work of God that enables particular people to recognize the presence of God in their lives and to receive and enjoy the gifts of God's grace. Pietist emphasis on the grace of God here and now, for me, in my personal experience, is inevitably emphasis on the Holy Spirit.

All Christians believe in the Holy Spirit, of course. But mainline Christianity has always been suspicious of too much talk about the Spirit.

For orthodox Christians who want above all to defend and preserve traditional patterns of thought and action, people who claim to have their own private revelations from the fresh outpouring of the Spirit mean the constant threat of heresy.

For theological liberals who are concerned about the renewal of society, people who claim to be filled with the Spirit are too preoccupied with the renewal of individuals and too tolerant of social injustice so long as they themselves are happy and blessed.

For leaders of the church establishment who want things done "decently and in order," people who claim to be guided by the Spirit are too unpredictable, too "emotionally unstable," too confident of their own spiritual superiority and therefore too disruptive and schismatic.

Even secular authorities who want law and order in civil society are wary of people who claim to have received the liberating power of the Spirit. They perceive such people to be more interested in freedom than in conformity and obedience, and they suspect that pious people who begin by fighting the devil in the hearts of individuals can easily become revolutionary fanatics who violently attack what they believe to be the work of the devil in the social order.

The history of the church shows that all these fears and suspicions are well founded. Beginning with the Corinthian church in the New Testament, and in every period of church history, people who get or think they have got the Spirit have often proved in fact to be heretical, socially irresponsible, self-righteous, fanatical troublemakers. But we need them. Or at least we need their irritating, disturbing, exciting, unrelenting reminder that to be a Christian means by definition to believe also in the surprising, revolutionary, liberating, empowering, and transforming work of the Holy Spirit—God's amazing grace at work not only in the distant past or somewhere else but right here and right now, not only in and for humanity in general but in and for *us,* beginning with *me.*

Criticism of Christian Pietism

Those whom orthodox and liberal Christians dismiss as "pietistic" come very close to the heart of Christian faith and life when they celebrate God's amazing grace and its consequences. But when we examine carefully their understanding of that grace, it becomes clear that they are not there yet.[1]

Pietism and the Biblical Understanding of Grace

Personal confession of sin, repentance, conversion, experience of God's saving grace, and enjoyment of all the present and future blessings it brings—all this is without question an important theme in both Old and New Testaments. But the same question we asked of liberal Christianity must be asked also of pietist Christianity: Is this the main theme, the heart, the primary goal of the biblical message? A careful reading of scripture reveals what a surprisingly small part of biblical history is devoted to stories about the personal experience of salvation, how individuals are changed by it and how they profit from it. Such stories are there, of course. We think of the stories of Abraham, Moses, the prophets, the disciples, and Paul on the Damascus road, all of whom had a direct personal encounter with God or Jesus that "turned their lives around." But such stories are there only as part of the larger and more important story of God's dealings with a chosen community of people and God's work through them for the welfare of all people. While such stories do speak of God's promises to help and protect, bless and save individual men and women, these promises are given to them not simply so that they may receive the gifts of God's grace for themselves but to prepare and empower them for the costly and dangerous task they are called to perform as agents of God's work in and for the world.

Throughout the Bible the main theme is this larger plan and work of God, and individuals' personal experience of salvation is secondary. But in the pietist understanding of Christian faith and life the main theme tends to recede into the background and the minor secondary theme takes center stage. Pietist Christians tend to believe in fact that the work of God is *limited* to God's activity in the lives of individual Christians, for their personal benefit. They tend to be uninterested in or even suspicious of the work of God's grace beyond their personal experience or in ways that threaten the fulfillment of their personal needs and desires.

All the other criticisms to be made of the pietist understanding of what it means to be a Christian are consequences of this tendency to misunderstand the purpose and scope of God's amazing grace as scripture proclaims it, giving first place to what has only second place in scripture, giving at best second place to what has first place in scripture.

Pietism and the Church

Pietist Christians tend to be indifferent or even hostile toward the church. Some believe that while the church may sometimes be useful to confirm and nourish their personal religious experience, it is not really essential. They believe that the saving and transforming grace of God comes just as well apart from the church through direct personal encounters with the Lord, through private prayer and Bible-reading, through the witness of an individual born-again Christian, or through fellowship with a few other such Christians. Other pietist Christians believe that the church actually hinders the experience of God's grace: The church's worship is a boring and dead routine devoid of any real sense of the presence of God. The church's preaching and teaching is halfhearted communication of religious truth by people who show no personal experience of or commitment to the great things they talk about. The sacraments are only empty rituals that make the service longer and delay Sunday dinner. The organization and programs of the church are ends in themselves, while the personal needs, problems, joys, and sorrows of individual Christians are ignored or stifled. The fellowship of the church is indistinguishable from that of any social or service club. The church's evangelistic efforts are more concerned with the size and budget of the church than with the salvation of the lost. The church, in other words, is made up of too many people, preachers and members alike, who are only "nominal" Christians. To listen to them and associate with them is to compromise one's own Christian experience, to deprive oneself of the warm fellowship of other real Christians, and to risk losing the joy and zeal of one's own authentic Christianity. Serious Christians, therefore, can only nourish their Christian faith and life by withdrawing altogether from the "organized" or "institutional" church to a purely private Christian existence or by forming independent small groups of truly born-again and committed Christians outside the church or perhaps as an elite little circle within the church.

How shall we respond to this criticism? Let us grant immediately that the pietist perception of the church is often painfully accurate and that the church needs to listen to it very carefully. So rather than trying to defend the church against these charges, we will focus instead on what pietist Christians do to themselves and their own cause with their indifference or hostility toward the church. In at least two ways they run the risk of cutting themselves off from the very saving and renewing grace of God that is so important to them.

1. In the first place, they risk missing the very personal divine guidance they seek. Pietist Christians tend to withdraw from the church to find in private or small-group Bible study the fresh, exciting, personally relevant word from the Lord they miss in the church's preaching and teaching. Personal or small-group Bible study is a good and necessary thing. But when people depend only on their own private interpretation of scripture, or that of a few other people like them, they risk finding in scripture not the Word of God but only the confirmation of their own wishes and opinions or those of the particular race, class, nationality, or religious group to which they belong. They risk being able and willing to hear just a few isolated passages of scripture that tell them only what they want God to say to them and do for them, and they risk being unable and unwilling to hear passages that challenge and correct rather than confirm their wishes, prejudices, and goals. Even more vulnerable at this point, of course, are those who want a direct word from the Lord or a direct inspiration of the Spirit without any guidance from scripture at all.

2. Second, when Christians withdraw from what they consider the dead or superficial life of the church, they risk losing the very personal benefits they seek. In their self-nurturing spirituality they tend to forget that the freedom, joy, and peace they seek is promised to the *community* of God's people as they give themselves to the costly and demanding task

of serving God and caring for others. They tend to seek ecstatic religious experience as an end in itself rather than as preparation for the great privilege of participating in the mission of the church in and for the world. Consequently they run the risk of confusing true and lasting freedom, joy, and peace with the false and temporary exhilaration, freedom from anxiety, and self-confidence that can come just as well from various self-help techniques or even from drugs or alcohol, sexual stimulation, listening to Bach or rock music, shopping, jogging, or any of the other ways we have of making ourselves feel good. They risk replacing true Christian blessedness with shabby imitations of it that are bound finally to leave them bitterly disappointed and empty.

Now of course the leaders and members of the church can make these mistakes too. But in the church there is a built-in safeguard against all narrow and self-serving interpretations of the meaning of scripture and Christian faith and life. This safeguard becomes apparent when we remember that the church is more than just a particular congregation, more even than just a denomination. It is the whole community of God's people made up of people all around the world who are culturally, racially, and nationally different from each other and who are guided and corrected by the church's struggle through the centuries to understand the truth, demands, and promises of scripture. For the sake of their own quest for the truth and grace of God, pietist Christians need the very plurality of past and present Christian insight and experience in the church they fear and condemn.

It is true as they often insist that the work of God's grace is not dependent on the church, that it can break into people's lives apart from the church. But pietist Christians' own Bible promises that the experience of God's grace will come especially in and through this all too human community, its inadequate and sinful preachers and teachers, its sacramental use of ordinary water and wine and bread, its often superficial fellowship, its often self-serving evangelism and missions, its tendency all too often to be more interested in organizational efficiency than in people. Those who are not willing to receive God's grace mediated through this human, worldly, sinful community refuse to hear God's own word about where and how it is encountered, recognized, and experienced. To the extent that they are so certain of their own superior wisdom and spirituality that they think they do not need the help, guidance, and possible correction of the church, they run the risk of blindness to the grace of God when it comes into their lives, and they risk missing the very guidance and gifts they want most.

Pietism and the World

A good example of the kind of one-sided reading of scripture to which
pietists are prone is the way they understand what the Bible tells us about
the relation between God's grace and the world. They like to quote New
Testament passages telling us that this world with all its earthly pleasures
and cares is passing away, that it is a wicked place in which Satan and
his forces of evil are powerfully at work to gain control over individual
people and over social and political structures. They like to quote Jesus'
saying that his kingdom is not about such things as food and clothing,
or the greed of worldly people for money and power. They like to quote
Paul's demand that Christians should not be conformed to this world but
transformed by the renewal of their minds in Jesus Christ.

But they tend to overlook other passages telling us that God so loved
this creaturely, wicked world that the Son of God came into it as a
human being to heal human hurts, share earthly joys and sorrows,
preach good news to poor people, suffer, and die for the *world's* salvation.
They overlook the fact that every time Satan and his demons of darkness
are mentioned in the New Testament it is to tell us about the defeat and
destruction of these false pretenders by the Christ who is the world's one
and only true Lord. They overlook the fact that Christians are commanded to reject the norms and values of the world and to be "different"
from other people not just for the sake of their own personal renewal and
transformation but for the sake of God's plan for a new heaven and earth.
They overlook the fact that the main theme of the Bible is not salvation
from the world but the salvation of the world, not escape from earthly
human existence but the fulfillment of it, not just the creation of Christians but the creation of a new humanity, not just the coming of personal
salvation to a few but the coming of the kingdom of God for the sake
of all.

The result of this one-sided reading of scripture is that pietist Christians tend to be so preoccupied with their private experience of God's
saving grace and their private enjoyment of it that they are uninterested
in the world around them. Or they tend to be so afraid that their own
moral purity, spirituality, and happiness would be destroyed by involvement in worldly affairs that they actually look at the world with suspicion and hostility.

This otherworldliness is usually criticized for what it does to other
people. Pietists are accused, for instance, of being so concerned about
their own and sometimes others' "spiritual" needs that they are uncon-
cerned about the "merely physical" needs of the poor and oppressed.
They are accused of actually contributing to social and economic injustice by their very indifference and silence in face of it. They are accused

of enjoying and thanking God for their own material security and comfort while at the same time condemning others who are concerned about such things for being "materialists" or "secular humanists." These accusations are often justified. But as in the case of our criticism of the pietist attitude toward the church, our criticism of pietist otherworldliness will focus on its unfortunate consequences for the faith and life of pietist Christians themselves.

To the extent that their one-sided reading of scripture prevents them from hearing the good news of God's love for the world, they undermine confidence in the work of God's grace in their own lives. Try as they might to enjoy the blessings of God in the safe isolation of their private lives, they cannot always avoid awareness of the suffering and injustice that plague their fellow human beings, some of them fellow Christians whose experience of personal salvation and trust in the Lord is just as genuine as their own. How long can Christians continue to believe that God cares about their own physical and spiritual needs if they do not believe that God also cares about all those other people out there? How long can they continue to believe in the power of God's grace over the demonic influences in their own lives if they do not believe that God's grace is stronger than the influence of Satan in the political and economic spheres? If they believe the devil is so strong that he can dethrone God to take over God's world, how long can they continue to believe that God can defend *them* against the powers of darkness?

Confidence in God's loving and powerful grace in our own lives stands or falls with confidence in God's loving and powerful grace in the world. Unless faith in the amazing grace of God includes faith in the sovereign power of God's grace in and over the world, we are doomed to lose confidence in that amazing grace in our own lives too.

Pietism and Christian Discipleship

Christians who sing "Amazing Grace" celebrate in a moving way all that God gives us and does for us, but there is not a word in this hymn about the claim God has on our lives. Of course Christians for whom this hymn summarizes the main theme of Christian faith and life know that along with the blessings bestowed by grace comes also the responsibility to serve God and other human beings. But for them the gifts God promises tend to be far more important than the tasks God assigns, and when they do think about the tasks, they tend to interpret them in such a way that they do not threaten enjoyment of the gifts. This results in a tendency severely to limit the meaning of Christian discipleship in at least three ways.

First, pietist Christians tend to limit the *extent* of Christian discipleship. Service of God tends to be limited to private devotional exercises or services of praise in small groups of like-minded Christians. Service of other people tends to be limited to acts of love and compassion in one-on-one personal relationships within the family and a small circle of others who are like them. Serving God and neighbor by participating in the fellowship and mission of the church is not high on their agenda. Nor is working for a more just social order that reflects God's rule of justice and peace for the benefit of all people in the world.

Second, pietist Christians tend to limit the *content* of Christian discipleship. "Love" is a much-used word in their Christian vocabulary. They correctly emphasize that Jesus summarized the whole of the law with the commandment to love God with our whole being and our neighbor as ourselves (pietists always put special emphasis on "as ourselves"). But they tend to pass over hard sayings of Jesus that make unmistakably concrete just what this love involves. They do not often talk about Jesus' warning that following him means putting commitment to the kingdom of God in the world above commitment to a warm and secure family life. Or Jesus' command to love our enemies, including those of our own race, class, nation, or religious group. Or Jesus' example of self-giving love that risks one's own purity, good reputation, and even safety to befriend sinners and outsiders who are excluded and rejected by good, law-abiding religious people. Or Jesus' warning that to love and follow him means willingness to sacrifice wealth and financial security for the sake of the poor and oppressed. Pietist Christians (and of course they are not alone!) tend to be all for love, so long as it does not threaten one's own self-interest, but to be silent about the self-sacrifice and self-denial that is the dangerous consequence of the universal and unqualified love Jesus taught and exemplified.

Finally, pietist Christians tend to have a limited view of the *purpose* of Christian discipleship. Ask them why they try to live as Christians, and the answer (like that of Christian moralists we discussed earlier) is likely to be "because it brings so much meaning and joy into my life," or "because I couldn't be happy unless I served the Lord and helped other people," or "because I couldn't live with myself otherwise." Listen to what they say when they appeal to others to become followers of Christ, and they are less likely to speak about the cause of God in the world or about the needs of other people than about the happiness, self-fulfillment, and freedom from guilt that come with being a Christian. Christian discipleship is there, but more because of what it does for the Christian's sake than because of what it does for God and other people. The task is there but only insofar as it contributes to the *rewards* for being a Christian. Service of God and neighbor tends to become self-service.

Behind all these limitations lies the concern to interpret Christian discipleship in such a way that it does not threaten but enhances Christian enjoyment of the happiness and inner peace, blessing, and salvation that are the gifts of God's grace. It is obvious that the cause of God in the church and in the world suffers from such a self-centered and self-serving view of discipleship. But once again we will focus on how the pietist version of Christian faith and life is self-defeating for pietist Christians themselves. With it they rob themselves of the full experience of what may be the greatest of all the gifts of God's grace—freedom.

Pietist Christians know from personal experience some things some other Christians know only theoretically about the great freedom that comes when one is saved by grace. They know about the freedom that comes when we give up the desperate compulsion to save ourselves by good works or just plain hard work and begin to live with the assurance that God accepts us just as we are. They know about the freedom that comes when we stop trying to carry our worries and problems by ourselves and lay our burdens on the Lord. They know about freedom to live with the wonderful joy, deep and abiding calm, and sure hope and confidence that come when we experience the personal comfort, security, and protection that come with God's amazing grace. But pietist Christians experience only part of God's gift of freedom if that is all they know about it.

Christian freedom is freedom *from* self-centeredness that is self-defeating and self-destructive even when it is pious self-centeredness preoccupied with one's own personal purity and salvation and the blessings that accompany them. It is freedom for the true self-fulfillment that comes when one centers one's life, not in oneself and one's own family and friends but in God and all our neighbors.

Christian freedom is freedom *from* remaining babies in the faith whose relations with others are determined by the gratification of their own needs and desires. It is freedom to grow into responsible Christian adults who know that they are not the center of the universe, who know that human life in general—and Christian life in particular—is often hard and painful, and who know that by the grace of God they will receive the strength and courage they need to live out their Christian faith in the real world.

Christian freedom is freedom *from* the trivial and fleeting joy and peace that result from superficial religion that promises (but cannot deliver) escape from the problems, hurts, and hardships others experience. It is freedom to discover the grace of God that helps Christians bear the problem, hurts, and hardships that inevitably come to them as to all other human beings. More than that, it is freedom to know the deep and abiding peace and joy experienced by those who for the sake of God and other human beings are willing to accept the *additional* problems, hurts, and hardships that come with faithful Christian discipleship.

Christian freedom is freedom *from* the inevitable disillusionment that comes with the false promises of religious consumerism, which differs from secular consumerism only in that the product to be "bought" to guarantee health, wealth, happiness, and success is "the Lord" rather than shampoo, patent medicine, the latest prestige automobile, Miller Lite, or Pepsi-Cola. It is freedom to discover the comfort and help God promises to those who are willing to risk health, wealth, happiness, and success for the sake of the rule of God's justice and peace in the world.

The weakness—the tragedy—of pietistic Christianity is that its followers (along with many other Christians) cheat themselves of this true freedom because they know too little about the amazing grace of God. To use the language of classical theology, they do not know that God's grace is both "justifying" *and* "sanctifying" grace. They know about justifying grace, which gives sinners free enjoyment of God's forgiveness, acceptance, love, and care. But they tend to be afraid of sanctifying grace (except insofar as it pays off in personal benefits) because it comes first in the form of hard demands and commandments that call Christians to subordinate their self-interest to costly discipleship and dangerous mission in both the personal and the political and economic spheres. What they do not understand is that these hard demands and requirements are *themselves* the gift of God's grace, given for our own good, to show us the way to life that is truly self-fulfilling just because it is free from all self-centeredness. What they do not understand is that with God's total claim on our lives comes God's promise to enable us freely and gladly to do what God requires of us. They do not understand the freedom that comes also with God's sanctifying grace. And the tragedy is that as long as they hold themselves back from unqualified discipleship and mission, they will never discover the amazing fullness of the amazing grace of God that makes people really free.

Pietism and the Holy Spirit

We said earlier that pietist Christianity is Christianity of the Holy Spirit. It is the presence and work of the Spirit that pietist Christians celebrate when they celebrate the amazing grace of God in their own personal experience, here and now. We recognized that this emphasis on the Spirit is one of the greatest strengths of this type of Christianity. But now we can summarize everything we have said about its weaknesses by speaking of its inadequacy just at this point. To the extent that pietist Christians limit the amazing grace of God to their own personal experience and enjoyment of it, they close themselves to the very gifts and power of the

Spirit that are so central to their understanding of what it means to be a Christian.

To the extent that pietist Christians expect to experience the grace of God apart from the *church,* it is not just the church but the Holy Spirit they ignore or reject. According to the New Testament, the Christian community is the first and primary result of the coming of the Spirit (Pentecost!). Where the Holy Spirit is at work, the church is born, built up, held together, instructed, led, and sent out on its mission to the world. Individual Christians receive the Spirit and the gifts of the Spirit not just for their own private enjoyment but for the upbuilding and equipment of the ministry of the church.[2] To the extent, therefore, that pietist Christians openly or secretly separate themselves from the church, they deprive themselves not just of the fellowship of other Christians but of the fellowship of the Holy Spirit. They deprive themselves not just of the mutual enrichment that comes from fellowship with Christians whose religious experience is different from theirs but of the mutual enrichment that comes in fellowship with Christians who have received the rich variety of the gifts of the Spirit. They deprive themselves not just of the church's teaching and preaching but of the truth into which Jesus promised the Spirit would guide the community of his followers. Insofar as pietist Christians think they can dispense with the church, they deprive themselves of the very gifts and power of the Spirit that can enable them to be the Spirit-filled Christians they so earnestly desire to be.

Second, to the extent that pietist Christians expect to experience the grace of God in escape from the *world,* with all its needs and problems, sin and suffering, it is not just the world but the powerful presence and work of the Holy Spirit they run from. The world may indeed be a world "with devils filled," but according to scripture it is also a world in which the Spirit of God is powerfully at work—above all to achieve *justice* for all those who in this world are poor, forgotten, excluded, exploited, and oppressed. According to the prophet Isaiah it is precisely the achievement of such justice that will be the work of the coming Messiah on whom "the Spirit of the Lord" will rest (Isa. 11:1–9; 32:14–16; 42:1; 61:1–9). And that was and continues to be the work of Jesus, who quoted Isaiah to explain who he was and what he came to do: "The Spirit of the Lord is upon me . . . to preach good news to the poor . . . release to the captives . . . sight to the blind, to set at liberty those who are oppressed" (Luke 4:18). To the extent, therefore, that pietist Christians flee the world and the battle for political and economic justice in it, they flee the very Holy Spirit they want to find. To the extent that they do not recognize and participate in the powerful work of the Spirit, wherever and by whomever justice is done for the sake of the powerless and dispossessed, they deprive themselves of the experience and assurance of one of the most amazing of all the manifestations of the spiritual power they love to talk about—power so great that not even the sinful world can stand against it.

Finally, to the extent that pietist Christians want to experience the grace of God by avoiding the difficulties of unreserved *discipleship,* it is not just the demands and commands of God but the Holy Spirit they ignore or reject. They deprive themselves of the very energizing, renewing, transforming power of the Spirit they bear witness to in their own personal testimonies to the work of the Spirit in the lives of Christians.

But all that is only the tip of the iceberg. The Holy Spirit is none other than God the creator, ruler and sustainer of the world, present and at work among us. The Spirit is none other than the presence and work of the living, risen Christ among us. To the extent that pietist Christians flee or resist the work of the Spirit in the church, in the world, and in faithful Christian discipleship, they are in danger of fleeing and resisting not just the Spirit but God the Father and God the Son as well. To the extent that they limit the work of the Spirit to the private enjoyment of their own salvation and spirituality, they are in danger of what Karl Barth once called "pious godlessness." They are in danger of being godless just because of their self-centered, self-seeking piety.

We should say immediately that the danger pietist Christians face is no greater than that faced by followers of other types of Christianity. Orthodox Christians are in danger of worshiping and serving the Bible or their orthodox theology instead of God. Liberal Christians are in danger of worshiping and serving their moral principles and political or economic ideologies instead of God. But the danger of pietistic idolatry, while not greater, may be more subtle and tempting than that of orthodox or liberal idolatry just because it is so "spiritual," just because it is in the name of the Holy Spirit that pietist Christians justify their devotion to themselves and their own present and eternal happiness and well-being.

"Amazing Grace" is a great hymn. It is a great thing for me to be found and saved, comforted and cared for, and promised good as long as life endures (indeed, for all eternity). But those whose favorite hymn and theme song is the amazing grace of God that saves *me* had better beware. They are only beginning to understand what it means to be a Christian, and if they do not move on to a deeper and more mature faith, they are in danger not just of losing but of rejecting the very amazing grace they celebrate.

Part II

Learning to Sing a New Song

Beyond Orthodoxy, Liberalism, and Pietism

What *does* it mean to be a Christian? In the following chapters we will talk about what it means in terms of a concept that I believe can combine the strengths and avoid the weaknesses of all the various types of Christianity we have discussed to this point. Although this concept is by no means a new way of understanding the meaning of Christian faith and life, I know of no hymn (no good one, anyway) that makes it a central theme, so at least in terms of hymnody it will demand a new song. The concept I have in mind is "witness." A Christian is first and last simply a witness to Jesus Christ.[1]

At first glance this idea does not sound very promising. The problem is not that "witness," "witnessing," "bearing witness," and related concepts such as "testifying" or "giving testimony" are difficult to understand or that they are outdated and meaningless terms to us who live in the "modern world." These words are commonly used, and everyone knows what they mean, in legal and business contexts. The problem is that such language has been so overused, misused, and trivially used in the religious sphere that many Christians as well as non-Christians react negatively when they hear it. It brings to our minds demented preachers on downtown street corners, or hard-to-get-rid-of door-to-door evangelists who interrupt our meals or TV programs with their memorized spiels and arguments, or religious hucksters on radio and TV telling us how healthy, rich, successful, and saved we will be if we will only turn our lives over to the Lord—and send in our contribution. We think about self-congratulating and self-advertising Christians at "testimony services" talking about how sinful and miserable they used to be and how holy and blessed they have become since they accepted Christ as their personal Lord and Savior. Or, more respectably but less interestingly, we think about a once-a-year money-raising time in the church called "witness season" or about church programs to train ministers and lay people in various evangelistic methods and techniques to increase church membership.

But the concept of witness or witnessing is too important for us to abandon. While it is not the only term that could be used to talk about what it means to be a Christian, I believe that it comes so close to the heart of the matter that it is worth reclaiming despite the difficulty of overcoming the distorted images it brings to our minds. That is what we will try to do in this part of the book. In chapter 5 we will speak about what it means for Christians to be witnesses to Jesus Christ. Then in chapters 6 and 7 we will discuss the content of this witness.

5

Christians as Witnesses to Jesus Christ

It is clear that something has happened when we no longer speak of Christians as orthodox believers, liberals, or pietists but as "witnesses." Witnesses are not another "type" of Christian to be set alongside the others we have discussed. When we talk about Christians as witnesses, we talk about them in a way that breaks out of all the categories we use to classify ourselves and other Christians. But that is just what we need to do if we are to overcome the differences that set Christians against each other and hinder the cause of the Christian gospel in and for the world. We need to discover an understanding of Christian faith and life that *all* Christians, whatever their theological tag, can claim for themselves. We need not another type of Christianity but an understanding of what it means to be a Christian that Christians of all types can accept and by which they are willing to let their own as well as others' faith and life be measured, judged, and corrected.

But can "witness" achieve this goal? Is it the best concept to achieve it? Why not some other concept? And what precisely does it mean to be a witness—specifically, a witness to Jesus Christ? The purpose of this chapter is to answer these questions.

Witnesses to Jesus Christ

According to Acts 1:8, the very last word of the risen Jesus to his disciples was the command to be his witnesses, beginning where they were "and to the end of the earth." This command announces the main theme of the whole book. Throughout Acts the primary task of Christians is to bear witness to the story of the life, the death, and especially the resurrection of Jesus and to the consequences of these events for Christian faith and life. The title "witness" itself is not often applied to Christians in the rest of the New Testament (though according to the first chapter of John's Gospel, John the Baptist, the first Christian, identified himself as a witness, and in John 15:27 Jesus tells his disciples that they are to be his witnesses). But it is clear that "witness" is what all the first Christians, including the writers of the Gospels and the letters, under- stood themselves to be and what they invited hearers of the gospel to become: witnesses in attitude, word, and action to what God has done, is doing, and promises to do in the crucified and risen Jesus of Nazareth, the living and coming Lord and Savior.[1]

The definition of Christians as witnesses thus meets one of the main requirements we have repeatedly identified for an adequate understand- ing of what it means to be a Christian: It is biblically based and it is broad enough to incorporate not just a part but the whole of what is called precisely the New Testament "witness" to Jesus. Moreover, this funda- mental biblical understanding of what it means to be a Christian pre- serves the strengths and corrects the weaknesses of orthodox, liberal, and pietistic Christianity.

Think first of what is involved in the concept of witness. It makes clear that to become a Christian is first of all to be given a task to fulfill, a job to be done. If *pietist Christians* understood themselves first and foremost as people called to this task, they could never be tempted to succumb to a self-centered and self-serving understanding of the meaning of Chris- tian faith and life in terms of blessings and gifts to be received and enjoyed for their own benefit. If *orthodox Christians* understood them- selves first and foremost as people called to be witnesses, they could never be tempted to understand the meaning of Christian faith and life only in terms of thinking right thoughts and believing correct doctrines. Both pietist and orthodox Christians would be open to learn what is right about the *liberal Christian's* understanding of faith and life: Being a Christian involves obedient response to an invitation and command to an action to be taken, a good word to be spoken, and "good works" to be done for the sake of a Lord who calls people to "bear witness" to him in attitude, word, and deed.

Think further of what is involved in obeying Jesus' invitation and command to be witnesses to *him*—witnesses to Jesus Christ.

The *orthodox* are right. To be a Christian is to accept and defend the truth that is revealed in the Bible and preserved in Christian tradition. But if they understood themselves first and foremost as witnesses to Jesus Christ, they would remember that the truth they are called to serve is a living person, not a system of doctrine, a confessional tradition, or even the harmonized teaching of the Bible *about* God or *about* Jesus. They would let their theology be shaped, not by speculation about what God can or must say and do, but by the history of what God actually has said and done, and promises to say and do, in the story of the Old and New Testaments with its center in the story of Jesus. They would remember that the truth is Jesus himself, truth that is bigger, higher, deeper, and broader than even the most orthodox attempts to understand it. They would be willing and eager to let their fallible, human attempts to comprehend the truth be constantly judged, clarified, and corrected by him who is the truth. As witnesses to Jesus Christ they could never become witnesses only to themselves and their poor orthodoxy.

The theological *liberals* are right. To be a Christian is to be a doer of the Word and not a hearer only. It is to obey the commands of God, follow the example of Jesus, serve the cause of God's justice, goodness, and compassion in the world. But if they understood themselves first and foremost as witnesses to Jesus Christ, they would never be tempted to point to themselves and how good and loving and wise Christians are; in attitude, word, and deed they would point to how good and loving and wise *he* is. They would never confuse service of God or Christ with service of abstract moral principles, ethical ideals, and conservative, liberal, or revolutionary political and economic causes and ideologies. Like the one to whom they are called to bear witness, they would subordinate concern for moral respectability and loyalty to every party or cause to the demands of God's loving and just will for the personal and social welfare of human beings in need. Moreover, if they understood themselves to be only witnesses, they could never fall first into the fatal arrogance and then into the inevitable despair and cynicism of those who think that *they* should or could "bring in" the kingdom of God. They would know that the job of being the world's judge, reconciler, and lord has already been taken by another and that all they are called to do is to announce and to participate in what *he* has already begun and will surely finish. They would know that they have to be responsible only for the faithfulness of their witness to the kingdom, not for the success of the kingdom itself.

The *pietists* are right. To be a Christian is personally to experience the salvation brought by Christ and to live in a personal relationship with him. But if they understood themselves as witnesses to Christ, their personal testimony to what they have experienced would always point to the one whom they have experienced, not to their religious experience as such. They would be concerned to advertise how great and wonderful God is, not how great and wonderful Christians are. They would speak and act as those who have come to know a Savior and Lord who is not just their private Savior and Lord, concerned only with their personal spiritual and material welfare, but who is Savior and Lord of the world, concerned about the spiritual and economic, social, and political welfare of *all* people. They would know that to be filled with the Holy Spirit is to be filled with *his* Spirit and to experience the joy, peace, and assurance that come in serving not their own but *his* interests. They would therefore gladly participate in the life and ministry of the church, despite the sinfulness of its leaders and members, because it is the community of people to whom Christ promised his Spirit and whom he promised to make the instruments of his saving and renewing work in the world.

What is a Christian? A Christian is first and foremost a witness to Jesus Christ. Why could not orthodox, liberal, and pietist Christians discover an underlying unity in their common commitment to this fundamental biblical understanding of what it means to be a Christian? Even with such a common commitment, of course, their witness would vary according to their different experiences of Christ, different personalities and gifts, different views of what is more and less important, different cultural backgrounds, and different circumstances in which they seek to be faithful Christians. That is one reason why true and effective Christian witness is always connected with the church. Individual Christians need the Christian community, in which there are other Christians who can correct the inevitable one-sidedness and short-sightedness of their particular point of view, say and do things they themselves cannot say and do, reach people they cannot reach. On the other hand, if the Christian community is to bear witness to all people, it needs this variety of Christian witness. Instead of being suspicious, jealous, or resentful of other Christians who bear their witness in ways different from our own, why should we not be grateful for them? Despite all the differences between us, we are called in our various ways to say and do fundamentally the same thing, because we are all called to bear witness in word and action to the same Christ.

But all talk about such unity and openness is only wishful thinking, of course, unless there is a common understanding of the fundamental content of Christian witness. There is no one way to talk about this, no one statement that can say everything that needs to be said, no one formula that will magically heal all the divisions among Christians. But all Christians—orthodox believers, liberals, and pietists alike—agree that witness to Jesus Christ is witness to his birth, life, death, resurrection, and promised coming again. For all Christians therefore it means first of all, and most simply, witness to the presence of God in the world.

Witness to the Presence of God in the World

Witness to Jesus Christ is witness to the earthly Jesus who was—and to the risen Jesus who continues to be—Emmanuel, "God with us." It is witness to one in whom God was—and is—not distant but near, not absent but present, not just occasionally but *always* near and present (Matt. 28:20). It is witness to one whom God has made not just Lord and Savior of Christians but Lord and Savior of the world, and thus to a God who is present and at work not just in and through Christians and their church but *everywhere* (John 1:9; 3:17; Eph. 1:15–23; Phil. 2:9–11). It is witness to a God who is always and everywhere present in the world. Consequently, genuine Christian witness is shocking, offensive, dangerous—and incredibly exciting and hopeful.

If all that Christians could say was that "there is" a God "out there" or "up there" who controls human destiny and sometimes intervenes in human affairs from the heavenly heights, people might or might not be interested and convinced but they would not be surprised, threatened, or excited. Many people with or without any particular Christian convictions can talk about a God who lives "up in heaven" but occasionally "comes down" to do miraculous things in the world. What makes authentic Christian witness unique, vulnerable, and powerful (but never boring) is that Christians dare to bear witness to a God who in the earthly and risen Jesus is *present*—always present—*in* the world.

Again, people might or might not be impressed and convinced if all that Christians could say was that there is a God who is present in the minds and hearts of Christians and their church and in the influence they are able to have in the world. Many religious people, non-Christians as well as Christians, claim to be people who have experienced the presence of God in their lives and announce that they are the instruments of God's word and work in the world. What makes authentic Christian witness unique, vulnerable, and powerful is that Christians dare to bear witness to the God who raised Jesus of Nazareth from the dead, without the cooperation and in fact despite the desertion of his followers, and made him to be the present and living Lord over all the powers and authorities of the world. They dare to bear witness to the God who in the risen Christ is still present and at work in the world even where there are no Christians and no church, even where Christians cannot or will not proclaim and serve God's cause in the world. Of course Christians believe that God is also present in them and their church. Of course they believe that God can and does work also through them in the world. But their Christian witness is not to their own presence in the world, or even to God's presence and work in and through them. They dare to bear witness—in attitude, word, and action—to a God whose presence and work are *not* limited to Christians, their church, and their sphere of influence—a God who is present and at work *everywhere,* even outside the Christian sphere.

When they hear *this* witness to *this* God, many people will object that it is either absurd or blasphemous to claim that God—if there is a God—is present in a world in which there is so much greed, cruelty, indifference to human need, injustice, and meaningless suffering.

Others will object that if God is present anywhere, it certainly cannot be in the "secular" world but only in a very limited "religious" sphere. And they would like to keep it that way. They are quite willing to let God (and Christians) tend to the private religious needs and feelings of individuals and to the ceremonies and rituals of the church, but they do not want God (or Christians) meddling in the political, social, and economic affairs of practical life in the "real world" or calling into question what they already know from "modern science" about what is possible and impossible in that world.

Even some who call themselves Christians will object to witness to the presence of God in the world. It threatens their monopoly on God: How can God care as much for all those unbelievers as for us believers? Or it suggests that God does not need us Christians: How can God be present and at work out there without the help of our preaching, good works, and efforts to improve the world?

All these objections share the happy or unhappy conviction that the world is by definition a godless and godforsaken place: God cannot be present there, at least not without Christians' support and help.[2] But authentic Christian witness dares to say, both to those who would like to but cannot believe it and to those who for one reason or another do not even want to hear it: It is not so. This world is *not* godless and godforsaken. It is a world in which God is present—always, everywhere. As unrealistic, impossible, offensive, threatening—and unbelievably hopeful—as it sounds, how can Christian witness claim anything else if it is witness to the life, death, resurrection, and promised coming of "God with us"?

How then should Christians go about this witness? Certainly by *talking* about Jesus Christ (as simply, openly, and unashamedly as the pietists talk about him). But our talk will be cheap and unconvincing unless we first bear witness to God's presence by the way we live in the world, outside the "religious sphere," *before* we begin talking religious talk, even when we do not mention God or Jesus and do not even consciously think about them. Christians bear witness to the presence of God in the world first of all in the following ways:

By the way they drive their cars on expressways, treat checkout clerks at the grocery store, pay attention to those who serve them by collecting their garbage or taking their order at restaurants

By the political programs and economic policies they support or refuse to support—especially when their stand threatens the self-interest of the particular political, racial, or economic group to which they themselves belong

By the way they keep hoping and working for change in people and institutions when others say that nothing can be done

By the way they are saddened or outraged by events that cause some others to rejoice and rejoice when some others are bitterly disappointed

By the way they remain calm when others panic and are deeply disturbed when others are complacent

By their indifference to whether they or the church gets the credit when the cause of justice, freedom, and peace is advanced, being just as glad when it happens as the result of others' efforts as when it happens as the result of their own efforts

By the way they experience in their personal lives the same joys and sorrows, successes and failures that others experience without congratulating themselves on their moral or spiritual superiority when life is good and without becoming sour and bitter when it is not

By the way they sometimes experience the same godlessness and godforsakenness others experience yet nevertheless, despite all the evidence to the contrary, keep on living by their faith that God is present in the world even so

Sooner or later someone will ask *why*. Why this strange attitude toward the value and dignity of human life—*all* human life, including the life of those who seem unimportant, useless, undeserving, or threatening to the self-interest of one's own class, race, or nation? Why this stubborn refusal to panic with those who think the world is hopelessly doomed, and this equally stubborn refusal to share the confidence of those who are sure that the world will be saved by this or that political or economic ideology, this or that new scientific or technological achievement, this or that militaristic or antimilitaristic crusade? Why this obstinate hope, when there seems to be no good reason for hope, and this sense of coming judgment when others think everything is going just fine? Why this anger or joy, confidence or disappointment, fighting or refusing to fight at such inappropriate times? Why, in short, this swimming against the stream of the optimism *and* pessimism, liberalism *and* conservativism, sour cynicism *and* dreamy idealism, fatalistic determinism *and* naive confidence in human goodness and freedom?

Then will come the time for explicit talk about God and God's presence in the world. And then such talk will be taken seriously—even by those who cannot or will not believe it.

But what is it that God is doing in the world? Where and how is God's presence recognized? How precisely can we bear witness to it? We have already begun indirectly to answer these questions, but now we must move on to answer them more explicitly. Witness to the presence of God in the world in Jesus Christ is witness to the suffering love of God (chapter 6) and to the liberating power of God (chapter 7).

We must not forget that Christian witness is first and foremost in the *church's* witness. The risen Christ commanded his *gathered* disciples to be witnesses to him. The whole of the New Testament arose from and is addressed to the *community* of Christians. True Christian witness is never only personal and private but is always a corporate witness. When in the following pages, therefore, we speak of "Christians," we always think not of isolated individuals but of people who speak and act as members and representatives of the church—a particular congregation, some particular denominations, the worldwide community of Christians called the "holy catholic church."

6
Witness to the Suffering Love of God

Witness to Jesus Christ is witness to a crucified Christ, and therefore to the presence of God in the world as a God of suffering love. Christians are people who by their attitudes, actions, and words bear witness to a loving God who as such is also a suffering God.[1]

Classical orthodox Christian theology has always been suspicious of talk about the suffering of God: The man Jesus may be weak, suffer, and die, but God *cannot* be weak, suffer, or die. God is by definition immortal, omnipotent, unchanging in power and glory; to speak of God's suffering is blasphemy and heresy. Classical theology therefore emphasized the powerful love of a powerful God. It taught us to look for and recognize the presence of God in the world when we see evidences of this powerful love at work. When problems are solved, needs met, hurts healed; when evil is overcome and good is vindicated; when there are happy endings—then we see signs of the fact that there really is a loving and powerful God who cares for us and the world. Conversely, classical theology has also led us to doubt the existence of such a God when these good things do *not* happen.

This orthodox view of God is not totally wrong, but it forgets that Christians do not learn the meaning of God's sovereign power by speculation about what God can and cannot, must and must not, be and do if God conforms to our idea of sovereign deity. We learn what it means by looking at God's self-revelation in Jesus Christ. Because the classical view ignores this self-revelation (at least at this point), it underestimates the very sovereign power of God that it wants to defend. According to scripture, God's loving power is God's power to be not only God *over* us but God *with* us. It is God's power not only to *overcome* but to *share* human weakness, failure, suffering, and even death. It is God's power to love not only as the great helper and savior who dwells in majestic splendor in the heavenly heights; it is also God's power to love as our friend, companion, and fellow sufferer in the deepest depths of our earthly human lives. It is God's power (not compromising or sacrificing but precisely proving and manifesting divine sovereignty) to be willing and able to be human as well as divine. In short, the powerful love of God is revealed not only in the victorious risen Jesus but also in the suffering and dying Jesus. And Christians recognize the presence of God in the world not only when they see signs of God's powerful triumphant love but also when they see signs of God's powerful *suffering* love.

How do Christians bear witness to this presence of God in suffering love? According to scripture, it is by bearing witness to God as the friend, companion, and fellow sufferer of those who are "poor and oppressed." Much attention has been given in recent years to the meaning of Christian witness with respect to those who suffer from economic and political poverty and oppression. In due time, we will speak about this also. But first we will speak about the meaning of Christian witness with respect to two other forms of poverty and oppression that plague all human beings, whatever their political and economic status. None of these three forms of human poverty and oppression can be neglected if Christians are to bear witness to the full extent of the suffering love of the God who lives in solidarity with suffering human beings.

The Suffering Love of God for Poor Oppressed Creatures

All of us human beings are "poor creatures" whose lives are shaped by biological, psychological, sociological, and historical influences that sometimes have a beneficial effect but can also threaten, cripple, and destroy. Even the healthiest and strongest of us can become sick or be hurt. All of us are more or less limited in our capacity for emotional growth and interpersonal relationship. Sooner or later (sometimes it seems too soon or too late), in one way or another, all of us die. It is not bad but good to be fragile, limited, finite creatures of God. Our whole story is not told, as some have held, by saying that we are born, we suffer, we die. Even the most threatened or handicapped life is seldom a life of unrelieved misery. Within the smaller or larger possibilities open to us, we all have moments, hours, days, even years of joy and delight in our creaturely existence. Nevertheless it is true that sooner or later all of us experience the defenselessness, pain, and death that Karl Barth called the "dark side" of the creaturely existence God has chosen to give us.[2]

God does not promise to save us from our creatureliness. Even in "the next life" God promises not salvation *from* but the salvation *of* our creaturely existence. God does promise, however, not to abandon us but to share the inevitable hardship, suffering, and death that go with our creatureliness. God knows how we feel, because God has been there. As one who in Jesus participated in human existence, God knows what it is like to be a creature who hurts and cries, who is disappointed and afraid, who fails, who is betrayed by friends and defeated by enemies. As the Father of Jesus, God knows what it is like to give up and lose an only son. As the incarnate Son dying on a cross, God has personally experienced the terrible reality of godforsaken suffering and death. Why did all this happen to "God Almighty"? Because God wills and is able to be the friend, companion, and fellow sufferer of those who experience the poverty and oppression of their creaturely fragility, limitations, and finitude.

And Christians are people who are called to bear witness to such great love—the *suffering* love—of such a great God—a *suffering* God. How do they do it?

First of all, Christians bear witness to the suffering love of God by the way they face the dark side of their own creatureliness and that of those nearest to them. Christians are not spared hardship, disappointment, sickness, pain, and death any more than anyone else. They testify to the love of God not by the way they are spared but by the way they bear these common human experiences. They too suffer, but they know that they do not suffer alone. They suffer with the certainty that God will not abandon them even when they walk through the valley of the shadow of death (Psalm 23), even when they experience the depths of hell itself (Psalm 139). We must be careful here. We do not have to be perfect witnesses, always cheerful, uncomplaining, sweet, calm, courageous, and optimistic. Like the psalmist and Jeremiah and Jesus himself, we too may express the same discouragement, outrage, fear, self-pity—the same feeling of godforsakenness—that all human creatures feel in the face of their own or their loved ones' suffering and death. But in the midst of and despite these normal human feelings, Christians bear witness to the suffering love of God not only for themselves but for all people by their assurance even in their godforsakenness that, nevertheless, "thou art with me."

Second, Christians bear witness to the suffering love of God by their willingness to risk sharing the creaturely poverty and oppression, suffering and dying, of *other people*. There are many reasons why we are reluctant to do this. We are too busy with our own problems and responsibilities. It is too painful and depressing. We hesitate to invade the privacy of others, especially the privacy of their suffering. We are afraid that we might hurt more than help because we might say or do the wrong thing. We feel guilty because we are so much better off and ashamed because we are secretly glad of it. We connect suffering with sin, and we cannot help but suspect that maybe "it's their own fault" and that "they brought it on themselves." The suffering of others is too brutal a reminder of the fragility and finitude of our own lives. We feel so helpless because we cannot heal the hurt or solve the problem.

But Christians are people who, despite all the good or questionable reasons for not doing so, risk sharing as best they can the troubles, hurt, loneliness, pain, and dying of other people. That involves first of all willingness to know about, see, and be exposed to the suffering and need of other people near at hand and far away. It means not protecting our own peace of mind by refusing to know and see and be exposed. It means not excusing ourselves because we "didn't know" but making it our business to find out. Then of course Christian witness means moving beyond knowing and seeing and feeling to personal involvement. It is not enough to tell ourselves and others how loving, compassionate, and sensitive we are because we are so touched and moved by all the suffering in the world around us. Christian witness requires actively initiating personal contact, establishing solidarity, sharing the burden with those who suffer—also when that means moving outside the familiar and safe circle of "our kind" of people. It requires support, including financial support, of other Christians and Christian communities who can be present in near or far places where we cannot be present ourselves. As, in Jesus Christ, God's love for the world is incarnate *present* love, so Christian witness to God's love can only be incarnate *present* witness.

Again we reach a point where we must be careful. While it is true, as many in our time insist, that Christian theology should be "incarnational" theology, this must not be interpreted to mean that Christians or the church are an "extension of the incarnation." We are not little Gods or Jesuses. We cannot and must not claim that we can or do demonstrate God's capacity for unwavering friendship, unqualified companionship, unlimited compassion. Such a claim can only lead finally to others' disillusionment, not only with Christians and the church but (far worse) with God. All we can and are asked to do is bear witness in our honestly acknowledged blundering and inadequate way to the suffering love of God, which is always far greater than the deepest or highest love we can ever achieve.

In some ways this is the easiest aspect of Christian witness to the presence of God in the world. We do not have to say the right words (not even the right theological words), give good advice, solve the problem at hand, accomplish anything, or pretend that our love and care are more than the limited human love and care they are. All we have to do is go there and be there and simply by our presence bear witness to those who suffer, that they are not abandoned and alone in their suffering, that not only a Christian but God is there as friend, companion, and fellow sufferer in the depths of their pain and sorrow.

The Suffering Love of God for Poor Oppressed Sinners

All of us are "poor sinners" who are oppressed not only by the dark side of our creatureliness but also by our sinfulness and its consequences. Our sin takes many different forms. There are "sins of the flesh," such as sexual promiscuity, drunkenness, and self-indulgence; and sins of the spirit, such as greed, envy, jealousy, hatred, and prejudice. There are sins of immoral, lawless people, such as lying, stealing, and killing; and sins of moral, law-abiding people, such as self-righteous unwillingness to forgive and care. There are sins of doing, desiring, and thinking; and sins of *not* doing, desiring, and thinking. There are sinful aggression and sinful passivity, sinful speaking and sinful silence, sinful disloyalty and sinful loyalty. There is the sinfulness of doing the right things for the wrong reasons; and the sinfulness of doing harmful and destructive things despite good intentions. There is sin that comes from choosing evil instead of good, from choosing the lesser of two evils, and from refusing to choose the lesser of two evils. There is sin committed in open defiance of justice, freedom, and truth; and equally terrible sin committed in the name of justice, freedom, and truth. There is sin that results from sacrificing the welfare of human community for the self-interest of individuals; and sin that results from sacrificing the welfare of individuals for the self-interest of the community. There is the direct sinfulness of deliberate choices we make as individuals; and the indirect sinfulness we share by virtue of the policies and actions of the economic class, race, nation, or church to which we belong. There is the sinfulness of unbelief that does not thank, trust, and obey God; and the sinfulness of belief that does so only in order to escape punishment and be rewarded. There is the sinfulness of people who hurt or ignore others; and the sinfulness of those who help others only to prove how loving they are and to bask in the warmth of being needed, thanked, and admired. There is the sinfulness of oppressors, the sinfulness of the oppressed, and the sinfulness of those who fight oppression. Sometimes we sin because, though we are able not to, we choose to; sometimes we sin because, though we do not want to, we cannot help it. Behind all these forms of sin and sinfulness lie our inability and unwillingness to love and let ourselves be loved in relation to God and other people. In one way or another all of us are trapped, trap ourselves, and are oppressed by our open or secret rebellion against God, our indifference or hostility in relation to our neighbors, and the resulting self-destruction of our own humanity.

But God is the friend, companion, and fellow sufferer of poor oppressed sinners. How do we know that? Because that is the way God meets us in Jesus Christ. The Jesus who was the friend of dishonest businessmen, revolutionary freedom fighters, prostitutes, heretics, and unbelievers—all kinds of unworthy and undeserving outsiders—that Jesus was *God* with us. If Jesus went into their homes, sat at table with them, invited them into the intimate company of his followers—then that is what *God* did and still does. If Jesus was willing to accept the righteous indignation and rejection of good, law-abiding religious people because of his friendship with such morally, spiritually, and politically questionable and unacceptable people—then that is what *God* is like.

Jesus did not permissively condone or indulgently excuse human sinfulness. He spoke hard words about the wrath and judgment of God against sinners (especially pious sinners) who did not love God and their fellow human beings. But if Jesus was willing to take on himself the judgment that falls on them, "pay the price" for their sins, suffer and die "in their place," bear in his own body the "chastisement" they deserved —then that is how *God* deals with guilty sinners. God is a just judge who is also a *loving* judge. A judge who is not against but for the condemned. A judge who takes up their cause, personally bears the pain of their sin and guilt, and suffers with and for them. A judge who exercises righteous judgment in such a way that it heals rather than hurts, forgives rather than gets even or pays back, reconciles rather than destroys, sets free rather than imprisons, grants life rather than condemns to death.

And Christians are people called to bear witness to the wonderful— and offensive—good news of the suffering love of this stern and strict lawgiver and judge who exercises judgment as the friend, companion, and fellow sufferer of poor oppressed sinners. How do they do it?

First of all, Christians demonstrate by their attitudes, actions, and words that they know *themselves* to be poor oppressed sinners who have experienced, and joyfully and thankfully accept, the friendship and companionship of God in the poverty and oppression of their own sinfulness. How can Christians bear witness to God as the friend of *sinners* if they present themselves to the world as those who are morally and spiritually superior to other people, thus contradicting their own witness by suggesting that God is not really on the side of sinners but on the side of good people like themselves? How can they bear witness to the great good news that God is the *friend* of sinners if they go around under a gloomy cloud of self-contempt and despondency because of their guilt and unworthiness, thus contradicting their own witness by suggesting that it is in fact possible to be so guilty and undeserving that one cannot count on God's friendship and forgiveness? Even before and apart from an explicit talk about the love of God, Christians bear witness to it by living as those who gratefully "accept their acceptance" (Tillich) and demonstrate in their attitude toward *themselves* that there is no sin so great that God cannot forgive it, no consequence of sin so painful that God will not be there to share it, no depths to which sinners can fall that God's love cannot reach them.

Second, Christians bear witness to God as the friend of sinners by their willingness as individuals and as a Christian community to risk the cost of befriending other sinners—all kinds of sinners. Sinners who are "our kind" and whom we are glad God loves, and sinners who are not our kind and whom we are inclined to suspect God does not and should not love. Christian and non-Christian sinners. Orthodox, liberal, and pietistic sinners. Red, yellow, black, and white sinners. Female and even male sinners. Sinners who are capitalists, socialists, and communists. Sinners who are the friends of our nation and sinners who are the enemies. Sinners who are poor and sinners who are rich or even middle class. Sinners who are oppressors and sinners who are the oppressed. Sinners who defend an unjust status quo, sinners who join in violent or nonviolent revolution, and sinners who say and do nothing at all in the face of injustice. Sinners guilty of "little sins" that are easy to forgive, and sinners whose sin is so great that many people think they deserve capital punishment. All kinds of sinners, guilty of all kinds of sin.

This friendship of Christians as witness to the friendship of God does not mean that Christians tolerantly overlook sin and make no distinction between right and wrong, just and unjust, what God requires and what God forbids. Like the God to whom they bear witness, they will confront and oppose every form of human sin that corrupts and destroys the good order God has established for the individual and corporate welfare of all human beings. But like the God to whom they bear witness, Christians do this not to get even, pay back, defeat, and wipe out the guilty sinners they oppose. They do it with the intention to help, restore, reconcile, and call even the worst sinners back to the true humanity God wills for them too.

Christians will inevitably get into trouble with such an attitude, of course. It leads them to seek out, sit down and talk and listen to, be seen in the company of, care about, and welcome into the Christian fellowship some people whom others consider immoral, ungodly, or politically and socially unacceptable. It means that like Jesus before them they themselves will be criticized for being immoral, ungodly, antisocial, or too liberal or too conservative. But unless they are willing to pay this cost, how can they be witnesses to a God of suffering love who is the friend of sinners?

Christians must be careful also in this aspect of Christian witness not to confuse or let themselves be confused with God. God's judgments are infallibly correct and just. God's capacity for understanding and compassion is unlimited. God is always perfectly just and perfectly loving at the same time. But when Christians condemn the sins of others, they can only do so as those who know, not just that they too are guilty sinners but that their personal sinfulness, or that of their race or class or nation, may be at least partly the *cause* of the sinfulness they condemn. When they judge others, they can only do so as those who know that their judgment is liable to error because they do not fully understand all the external and internal pressures that have contributed to the sins of those they judge. When Christians seek to befriend others who are sinners, they cannot do so as the strong and innocent who magnanimously condescend to be nice to the weak and guilty, but only as fellow sinners who know that they are just as much in need of God's gracious forgiveness and acceptance as anyone else. When they try to be both loving and just in dealing with others, they will be modest about the success of their attempt and open to correction, knowing that they always tend to choose justice at the expense of love, or love at the expense of justice, and thus tend to be neither truly just nor truly loving. They will make it clear in attitude, word, and action that they know their justice and love are at best only a pale reflection of God's justice and love. They can only do their best to bear witness to the God who *alone* is able and willing to be the truly just and truly loving friend, companion, and fellow sufferer of poor sinners oppressed by their sinfulness.

The Suffering Love of God for the Politically and Economically Poor and Oppressed

In some circles today this aspect of God's love has been emphasized so exclusively that the impression is given that God loves *only* those who are politically and economically poor and oppressed. It was partly to counter such one-sidedness that we have emphasized the love of God for those who are poor and oppressed in the creatureliness and sinfulness common to all human beings, rich and middle class as well as poor, oppressors as well as oppressed, powerful majorities as well as powerless minorities. Christian witness is witness to a God who loves *all* people, all of whom are poor and oppressed in one way or another. But having expressed this universal love of God as strongly as possible, we would not be true to the biblical witness if we did not go on to speak just as strongly of God's suffering love quite specifically for those who are poor and oppressed in the most obvious and concrete sense, not just in their general human neediness but in their political and economic neediness.

According to both the Old and New Testaments, the God to whom Christians are called to bear witness is the God who is especially on the side—*at* the side—of those in the world who are weak, defenseless, and destitute, victims of the indifference and injustice of the rich and powerful. God is the God who chose and still chooses to be the God of the Jews, a community of people who from the beginning and throughout history have with rare exceptions always been a rejected, excluded, despised, mocked, and persecuted people among the other peoples of the earth. That God is the God who through the prophets of Israel took up the cause of widows, orphans, and aliens—people without civil rights and representatives of all those who are the most vulnerable, helpless, and forgotten people in every society. That same God is the God who came to us in one who though he was rich became poor (2 Cor. 8:9), with "nowhere to lay his head" (Luke 9:58)—a man who came not for the sake of the rich and mighty but for the sake of the lowly and hungry (Luke 1:52–53), who promised the kingdom of God to the poor (Luke 6:20), who repeatedly warned against the corrupting influence of money and power (Luke 16:19–31; 18:18–25), who identified himself with the "marginal" people of society and was himself weak, rejected, despised, and finally killed by political and religious leaders who had power and influence.

To be a Christian, then, is to bear witness to such a man and such a God, a man and a God who are the friends and companions of those who are politically and economically poor and oppressed. How can we do it?

It is better if we do not speak too quickly of what those of us who are comparatively affluent and powerful should say and do. We ought first gratefully to acknowledge the witness of brother and sister Christians who are themselves poor and oppressed. Some of them bear witness to the presence of a loving God in the depths of human need and suffering by the way they live with dignity, courage, and moments of amazing cheerfulness and hope even in their desperate deprivation. Some bear witness to God's self-giving love by their astounding generosity in sharing the very little they do have with others who are in need. Some bear witness to the love of God for *all* people by the totally unexpected way they resist those who cause or permit their poverty and suffering without hatred or lust for vengeance. They understand how impoverished their oppressors themselves are by their slavery to their possessions, how dehumanized they are by their desperate competition with other people to get to the top and stay there, how oppressed they are by their compulsive quest for comfort and security, how great is their need to experience the reconciling and freeing love of God in their lives.

We more affluent Christians also need such a witness—we who tend to doubt the presence of God in our lives when God does not give us everything we need or want, who tend to be generous only to the extent that it does not threaten our own well-being, who are prone to seek the destruction rather than the reconciliation of our enemies. We often think of how the poor and oppressed need *our* help; we often forget how much we need the help of some of them to remind us what the Christian faith looks like when it is actually practiced.

But of course we more affluent and comfortable Christians are also called to bear witness to God's love for the poor and oppressed. How do we do that? It is important to remember that at this point in our discussion we are thinking about Christian witness to God's presence in the world as a God of suffering love, not yet about witness to God's liberating power. In the present context the question is not what we have to say and do to bear witness to God's work to overcome poverty and oppression; the question is what we have to say and do to bear witness to God's *presence* with the poor and oppressed *in the depths* of their suffering and need. The task of Christian witness from this perspective is not to discover how we can "save" the victims of poverty and oppression; it is a far more modest, less heroic, and in some ways more difficult task—to discover how we can *establish solidarity* with them, be their friends, companions, and fellow sufferers in such a way that we bear faithful witness to the God who is their true friend, companion, and fellow sufferer.

How then should we set out to fulfill this task? Without attempting to be exhaustive, we mention four things that more comfortably situated Christians can do.

1. In daily conversations with "our kind" of people we can speak up for the victims of poverty and oppression. When middle-class or wealthy people talk about homeless street people, or recipients of social welfare and food stamps, or the poor and dispossessed in other countries who rise up violently against their oppressors or flee them to seek refuge in our country, someone is sure to blame the victims. They are accused of being lazy, immoral, incompetent, irresponsible, worthless, undeserving, inferior, greedy, politically dangerous (probably communists), and so on. We can bear witness to the God who is on the side of "those people" by putting in a good word for them. Perhaps it will be to correct commonly accepted myths with facts. Perhaps it will be to observe that the faults and sins that are in fact to be found among "them" are not totally unknown among people like "us." Perhaps it will be to point out that the disadvantages and lack of opportunity connected with place of birth, family background, and race and culture have something to do with what "they" are and what they can and cannot accomplish—just as unearned privileges, advantages, and opportunities connected with place of birth, family background, and race and culture have something to do with the character and achievements of those of us who are better off. Perhaps it will be to counter the platitude that "God helps those who help them-

selves" with the good news that God also helps those who *cannot* help themselves. Perhaps it will be to point out that no matter how immoral, undeserving, worthless, unimportant, socially useless, or politically dangerous some people seem to us, they are nevertheless human beings created in the image of God and for that reason alone are due such basic necessities that sustain human life as food, clothing, shelter, basic education, medical care, and the opportunity to make a living for their families. In one way or another we bear witness to the God who is for the poor and oppressed simply by daring to speak up on their behalf (with or without any explicit talk about God or Christ).

But as important as such talk is, it is cheap talk unless we put our money where our mouth is. So: (2) We can give money to support Christian and secular groups at home and around the world that minister to the immediate needs of the poor and oppressed by means of night shelters, soup kitchens, medical clinics, sanctuaries for refugees, and other forms of emergency aid. Charitable work to alleviate suffering and need provides only temporary help. It can be only a bandage to cover a cancer. It does not threaten unjust political and economic systems and structures that are the underlying cause of poverty and oppression. Indeed, charity can be used as an excuse for *not* challenging social injustice and can even be a means of preserving unjust social situations. But for people who do not have, and cannot earn, enough money to pay for food, clothing, and health care for themselves and their families, "only money" given to provide for their immediate needs can be literally a daily matter of life and death. How can we bear witness to the friendship and companionship of God for such people if we are not willing to give up a little of our financial security for them?

But donating money can become a way of paying others to bear our Christian witness for us. So: (3) As individuals and Christian communities we can take the initiative personally to befriend the "poor and oppressed" as human beings with their own names and faces and their own human stories. Not leaving it up to others, we ourselves can participate in or help organize the ministry of night shelters, soup kitchens, medical clinics, day-care centers, places of sanctuary, neighborhood associations, and other forms of face-to-face care for suffering and needy people. The problem of poverty and oppression is one of such staggering worldwide dimensions that our tendency is first despairingly then complacently to decide that we can do nothing about it. But we can make ourselves the friends and companions of *some* of the wretched of the earth. If we do not befriend those we can see and know, how can we bear witness to the suffering love of the God who is present and at work, not just everywhere in general but here, where we live?

Everything depends on how we do it. Our acts of solidarity with the poor and oppressed must be acts of genuine solidarity, not acts of benevolent paternalism (or maternalism!). We tend consciously or unconsciously to approach them as superiors to inferiors, the strong to the weak, saints to sinners, the wise to the ignorant and foolish, with the insulting and condescending attitude, "We want to help you, you poor things." In dealing with "those poor unfortunate people down there below us," we tend to think (as orthodox Christians tend to think in dealing with those whose theology is different from theirs) that we can speak without needing to listen, advise and instruct without needing to learn, help without ourselves needing to be helped, correct without ourselves needing to be corrected, decide for them what we think they need most without letting them tell us what they think they need most (we might be surprised!). To the extent that this happens, it is no wonder that the poor and oppressed resent rather than welcome the "help" of Christians and their God. There can be no true solidarity with them unless we know and openly confess also in this context that we are not little saviors and lords but only fellow human beings who in our own way are just as finite, sinful, needy, and oppressed as they. There can be no witness to the true solidarity God establishes with needy and suffering humanity unless we follow the Christ who refused even benevolently to lord it over people, but made their poverty and weakness his own.

But even that is not enough. We inevitably convey the superior attitude we have just condemned if we associate with the poor and oppressed only in places where they go to receive tokens of our compassion. So: (4) We richer and more powerful Christians can welcome them to be with us where *we* live, inviting them into the daily and weekly fellowship of "our" church. How can we do otherwise if we are faithful to our own confession that the church of Jesus Christ is a community in which people of all nations, races, classes, and cultures come together, not as enemies or competitors, or even as dispensers and recipients of charity, but as brothers and sisters of the same household?

A popular theory of church development tells us that people have a "natural affinity" for other people like themselves and a natural aversion to people who are different. Therefore, churches will grow only if we intentionally build "homogeneous" congregations, each of which is made up of people of the same economic, racial, national, and cultural background. There would thus be a separate church for "upper" and "lower" classes, for the educated and the uneducated, for different ethnic groups. These congregations should of course support each other and occasionally worship together, but their members would not be called to intimate association with others who are not like them.

Everything the church says and does in behalf of the poor and oppressed will be rightly criticized as cheap, patronizing, and hypocritical if we follow this strategy and imitate secular culture in this way. The God to whom Christians are called to bear witness is a God who reconciles and includes, not a God who divides and excludes. How can Christians and Christian churches bear witness to such a God if they do not struggle with the admittedly difficult task of becoming an *unnatural* community in which poor and rich, powerful insiders and powerless outsiders, live in fellowship with each other? If we are not willing to risk popularity and numerical growth to become such a community, how can we bear witness to the Christ who not only went out to the poor and outcast but invited them to come in to him, who not only sought out their company but welcomed them into his company and the company of those who confess and belong to him?

All four of the forms of Christian witness we have mentioned point to the costliness of bearing witness to the love of God for the poor and oppressed.

This witness is costly to Christians' self-understanding. It means giving up all open or hidden pretense that we are the noble helpers of the helpless. It means acknowledging our own as well as their vulnerability and helplessness.

This witness is costly within the family circle. It leads Christians to express attitudes, make commitments, and say and do things that may embarrass, irritate, and even anger or alienate spouses and parents and children, not to mention in-laws (Matt. 10:34–39).

This witness may be costly even in the church and will certainly be costly in the public arena, where political and economic theories and strategies are debated. It means being accused of being too "literalistic" or too "unspiritual" in biblical interpretation, too liberal, too idealistic, too unrealistic, too "pink," too corrupted by "secular humanism" on the one hand or "utopian religion" on the other. It means that Christians will meet criticism and opposition from "good" as well as from "bad" people. It may even mean that we too could actually be persecuted as many other Christians have been in the past and as many other Christians in other parts of the world are today. (We must not forget that the New Testament Greek word for "witness" corresponds to our English word "martyr.")

This witness may even mean having to endure the initial suspicion and hostility of the poor and oppressed themselves, who have so often been manipulated and betrayed by people both on the right and on the left who claim to be on their side.

It is costly to bear witness to the love of God for those who suffer from the indifference and injustice of those who are rich and powerful. How could it not be, since it is witness to a Christ who identified himself with the excluded and rejected of the earth, who was hated and finally crucified for their sake, who warned his disciples that they too would be hated by all for his name's sake (Matt. 10:22) and told them to take up their own crosses to follow him (Matt. 10:38)? Unless we are willing to pay the cost of sharing his solidarity with the victims of poverty and oppression, how can we bear witness to a God of suffering love who is present and at work in the world as their friend, companion, and fellow sufferer?

7
Witness to the Liberating Power of God

Witness to Jesus Christ is witness to a God who is present and at work in the world not only as a God of suffering love but also as a God of liberating power. It is witness to the God who in the earthly Jesus and in the risen, living, and coming Lord Jesus Christ was and is and will be at work to free humanity and the world from sin, injustice, suffering, and death.

If we are to speak truly and realistically about Christian witness to this second way God is present in the world, we must avoid two mistaken ideas about the relationship between God's liberating power and God's suffering love.

The first mistake is to think that when we come to talk about the liberating power of God revealed especially in the resurrection of Jesus, we can now forget about the suffering love of God revealed in the crucified Jesus. As if once we have got beyond the gloom and doom of Holy Week to the joyful celebration of Easter Sunday we can speak only of a God whose real function after all is to solve our own and others' problems, heal our hurts, satisfy our material and spiritual needs, straighten out (or help us to straighten out) everything that is wrong in the world, and enable us to live happily ever after. But this "triumphalism," as it is called in the history of theology, is not biblical. We are quite right when on Easter Sunday we sing (with full organ, blaring trumpets, and massed choirs) about the risen Jesus who is "King of kings and Lord of lords" and who will "reign for ever and ever" now that "the kingdom of this world is become the kingdom of our Lord and of his Christ." But the New Testament is very realistic in acknowledging what we experi-

ence on the Monday *after* Easter and during the rest of the year: All the
sin, suffering, injustice, and death that have plagued our world in the past
are still there, and the world usually looks like the same old godless and
godforsaken place it seemed on Good Friday. Even after Easter, the
victorious risen Lord continues to be a weak, despised, and rejected
suffering servant in the world. He continues to be the same Jesus who
in self-giving love suffered and died for sinners and outsiders. He is a
risen Lord who must still be recognized and proclaimed as Christ crucified (1 Cor. 2:2). Jesus' resurrection means the promise and assurance
of the *final* victory of God's liberating power. But in the meantime God
continues to be present in the world as a God of suffering love, the friend,
companion, and fellow sufferer of those who in this life, in this world,
still remain victims of creaturely, sinful, economic and political poverty
and oppression. It is a mistake for Christians to bear witness to the
liberating power of God in such a way that they expect, or lead others
to expect, that it *replaces* the suffering love of God.

But the second mistake is just as bad as the first. It is to think and
speak and live as if Easter never happened at all, to be so convinced of
the invincible power of sin, injustice, suffering, and death that we give
up all confidence in the liberating power of God (at least in present
experience in this world) and expect God to be present (if at all) only
to comfort and sustain us in our weakness, need, suffering, and dying.
That is not biblical either. The first Christians bore witness to their actual
experience of the historical event of God's great victory over all the
powers of evil with the resurrection of Jesus. The early Christian community was held together by its weekly celebration of the liberating power
of God that had actually been demonstrated on the first Easter (for the
early Christians, every Sunday was celebrated as Easter Sunday). Moreover, even as a small and persecuted minority, they repeatedly experienced the renewing and transforming power of the risen Christ in
their individual lives, in the church, and even in the world around them.
They identified it as the power of the Holy Spirit bringing light where
there had been darkness, freedom where there had been bondage, faith
where there had been ignorance and unbelief, health where there had
been sickness, reconciliation where there had been alienation, steady
growth even in the face of brutal opposition. They were realistic about
the continuing reality of sin, suffering, injustice, and death in their own
lives and in the world. They still counted on God's comforting and
sustaining presence in their weakness, sinfulness, and need. But even so
they bore witness to the signs of the liberating power of God breaking
into their lives and into the world here and now—signs that meant the
promise of more to come. Complete and final liberation from creaturely,

sinful, political and economic poverty and oppression remained a future hope and not a present reality. But they were sure that hope for that complete and final liberation was not just wishful thinking or utopian dreaming because they remembered what God had already done in their past and because again and again, in limited, provisional, and partial but real ways, they continued to experience God's liberating power in their daily lives. It is thus a mistake for Christians to be so "realistic" about the godlessness and godforsakenness of the world that they can bear witness to the liberating power of God only when they think about the "next life" or "the end of history."

In identifying these two mistaken ways of relating the liberating power and the suffering love of God we have also identified the criteria for honest and faithful witness to the God who is present and at work in the world both as a God of suffering love and as a God of liberating power.

1. Authentic Christian witness to the liberating power of God is unflinchingly honest about the godlessness and godforsakenness we experience in our own lives and in the world around us. It does not ignore or piously explain away all the painful and shameful personal experiences and political and economic realities that challenge and threaten faith in the saving power of God.

2. Therefore authentic Christian witness to the liberating power of God will always continue to include witness to the suffering love of God as friend, companion, and fellow sufferer of individuals and groups in their need, guilt, suffering, and death. It will always continue to be witness to the truth about God revealed in the defeated crucified Jesus as well as in the victorious risen Jesus, witness to the good news of Good Friday as well as of Easter Sunday.

3. Authentic Christian witness to the liberating power of God is based on what God actually has done and still does in personal human experience and in human history. It is not based on speculation about what God must or could or should do or on guesswork or wishful thinking about what God might do. Specifically, it is based on the "mighty acts of God" in the life, death, and resurrection of Jesus and on repeated present experiences of the renewing and transforming work of the Spirit of the risen Christ, who even now is at work in and beyond the Christian community.

4. Therefore, authentic Christian witness to the liberating power of God always takes the form of witness to Christian *hope for the future*—hope that stubbornly persists despite the continuing presence of sin, suffering, injustice, and death in personal experience and in world history. This hope is hope not only for the little partial liberations that continually break into individual lives, the Christian community, and

political and economic realities as "down payments" (Eph. 1:14) on the great final liberation to come, but also for the final and complete victory of God's liberating power that is the end and goal of individual human life and of world history.

5. Just because Christians are sure that God is and will be more powerful than everything that spoils and destroys human life in God's world, authentic Christian hope for the liberating power of God cannot be passive and quietistic. It can only be active and aggressive. It is hope that enables and requires Christians in attitude, action, and speech to condemn and resist all resigned acceptance or conservative defense of "the way things are" in a world in which people are hurt, hurt themselves, and hurt other people. It is hope that leads Christians confidently to expect and work for change (sometimes radical change) in individual lives, in the church, in social institutions, and in political structures so that the life, freedom, justice, reconciliation, and peace God wills for all people will begin to be visible here and now. Moreover, Christian hope is hope that "infects" other people and encourages and empowers them to join in the struggle for the new humanity and the new world that the liberating power of God is already at work to create and will create.[1]

The significance and implications of these criteria will become clearer when we apply them to Christian witness to the liberating power of God in relation to the three forms of human poverty and oppression we discussed in chapter 6.

The Liberating Power of God and Poor Oppressed Creatures

The God we have come to know in the life, death, resurrection, and promised coming of Jesus Christ is the God who is and will be at work in the world, not only as a God who understands and shares but also as a God who *liberates* human beings from the poverty and oppression of their creaturely lives. This God brings and promises to bring bodily and mental health where there is sickness, physical and emotional wholeness where there is brokenness, growth where growth seems impossible, life where there is death. Of course God's liberating power does more than that. It brings salvation from sin and guilt and their consequences and reconciles sinners to God and each other, now and for all eternity. But we have not heard all the good news of the New Testament if we do not also hear the good news of this less "spiritual" way the liberating power of God is at work in the world. Christians bear witness to it by bearing witness in attitude, action, and word to their hope for liberation from creaturely poverty and oppression, both in the present and in the future.

Hope for Life in the Present

All human beings are vulnerable to physical, mental, and emotional handicaps, sickness, and suffering. All of us die. That is how God created us. That is what it means to be limited, finite creatures. God does not free us from the vulnerability, limitations, and finitude that are part of creaturely life. But God does protect and defend present human life *within* its creaturely limits. A blind person sees, or sees a little better, or finds that other senses are sharpened to compensate for not seeing. A deaf person hears, or hears a little better, or learns to communicate without hearing. A crippled person walks or learns to be independent without walking. A sick person is given many or a few more months or years to live. A severely retarded or injured person smiles or says a few words or learns a new physical skill for the first time. Whether the possibilities of human life are extended in great or small ways (small ways can be just as important and meaningful as great ones), the lives of all such people are still limited, sometimes very limited. Sooner or later they too will die. But Christians recognize all such partial, temporary extensions of human life and wholeness as signs of the full, whole, enduring humanity God intends for every person and for all people in the future.

We might think of a number of ways Christians can bear witness to this hope for the liberating power of God here and now, but we will speak of only two of them.

In the first place, we bear witness to hope for the liberating power of God by thankfully *acknowledging and expecting* the work of God in and through doctors, nurses, technicians, and institutions that provide medical and psychological health care. The risen Christ or the Spirit of God is at work in the doctor's office as well as in the pastor's study, in hospitals as well as in churches, through science and technology as well as through prayer meetings, in predictable and explainable ways as well as in unpredictable and "miraculous" ways, in and through unbelievers as well as believers. Whenever and however healing happens, in little or in great ways, Christians acknowledge the life-giving power of God at work. How could we bear witness to the great power of God if we spoke and acted as if it could be operative and effective only in a "religious" but not in a "secular" setting? How could we bear witness to the great power of God if we spoke and acted as if we really meant only the power of Christians, their faith and prayer or their specifically Christian healing ability?

Some professional healers with their medical and psychological skills (like some nonprofessional healers with their faith and prayers and religious rites of healing) sometimes refuse to acknowledge the limits of human creaturely life. They try frantically to heal sick, handicapped, or injured people who can only be accepted, loved, and cared for as they are. They desperately or too matter-of-factly use mechanical techniques to preserve creaturely life that has come to its end. When this happens, human healers become rivals rather than instruments of God. Even with the best of wills it is not always easy to recognize the point at which defending and maintaining creaturely life becomes refusal to acknowledge its limits. But the fact that this boundary can be violated does not alter the fact that Christians can gladly expect and point to the liberating work of God in legitimate human efforts to provide health and wholeness for God's creatures.

If this witness is to be faithful, and if it is to be taken seriously by others, Christians must do what they can as individuals and as Christian communities to support programs of public and private health care for all people, regardless of race, religion, moral worthiness, or ability to pay. The question of universal health care is not just a question of conservative or liberal political and economic ideology. It is the theological question of whether we really believe in the liberating power of the God who in Jesus Christ cared for and still cares for the physical and emotional, as well as the spiritual, welfare of *all* human beings. It is the question of whether we really believe in the Holy Spirit, the "Lord and Giver of Life" (Nicene Creed) for *all* God's creatures. It is the question of whether we are faithful witnesses to our own proclamation of hope in the healing power of the God who is the creator and sustainer of *all* life.

In the second place, Christians bear witness to the liberating power of God by *praying* both for themselves and for others in affliction, illness, and the threat of death. Prayer is no excuse for laziness and irresponsibility in doing what we can to care for ourselves and for others. But if we really believe in the healing power of God, how can we not bear witness to it by praying for ourselves, praying with and for others, and letting it be known that we pray?

We speak with good reason of the "problem" of prayer. Does it make any difference? Does it work? Does God hear? Does God answer? If God already knows what we need, why should we pray? Does prayer change God or only change our attitude about what happens to us? We can keep asking questions forever. But it is not necessary to solve all these problems and answer all these questions before we begin to pray. It is the power of *God,* not the power of our understanding or faith or the power of prayer itself, that enables us to pray. We pray simply because God has invited and commanded us to do so and has promised to be influenced by our prayers. Because of this invitation, command, and promise we may go ahead and pray despite our unanswered questions, our doubts, our shaky faith, our unworthiness to ask anything of God—despite all the good reasons we can think of for not praying. The important thing is that we do it. As simply and directly as children expressing their needs and desires to their earthly parents. Without worrying whether we use the right words or do it "correctly." Without any particularly pious attitude or tone of voice.

And God does answer. Sometimes we get what we want, even when it seems medically improbable or scientifically impossible. Sometimes our requests are not granted. But the answer is always "yes" to *us* even when it is "no" to what we ask for. Like a good parent, God sometimes refuses to give us what we want and think we need, in order to give us what is best for us in the long run. God said "no" to Jesus' prayer to be spared the humiliating and violent death that was approaching, but through that death came the realization of the kingdom Jesus had given his whole life to proclaim and inaugurate. God said "no" to Paul's earnest request for the removal of the "thorn in the flesh" that deeply troubled him, but instead God gave Paul something even more important, the grace that enabled him to fulfill his life's work despite "weaknesses, insults, hardships, persecutions, and calamities" (2 Cor. 12:7–10). (We may note in passing that God's "no" to Jesus and Paul was given to people with unquestionably great faith. When prayers are not answered as we wish, that does not necessarily mean that we do not have "enough faith." Faith is not the means by which we get God to do for us and give us what we want; it is willingness and ability to recognize God's presence in our lives even when that does not happen.)

Christians, then, bear witness to the power of God (not the power of prayer) by praying for themselves and others in sickness, affliction, and threat of death. They do not expect or encourage others to expect God's power to do away with all the God-given limitations of creaturely life. But by their prayers they bear witness to hope for the liberating power of God *within* those limits—sometimes to increase the possibilities of life, sometimes to make life more intensely meaningful and valuable within a very narrow range of possibilities. To be a Christian is by definition to pray and in this way bear witness to confident Christian hope for the liberating power of God to be at work in one way or the other, here and now.

Hope for Life in the Future

Christian hope is hope for the life-giving power of God, not only within but over and beyond the limits of human life in this world. It is hope for the power of God that will liberate all human beings from the suffering and death that are a built-in part of their creaturely existence. It is hope for a future in which there will be no more mourning, crying, pain, or death for anyone, anywhere (Rev. 21:4). It is hope, in other words, for "life after death." Christians are people who bear witness to this hope.

If our witness to it is to be both faithful and relevant, we must distinguish authentic Christian hope from some common distortions of it that come from within as well as from outside Christian circles.

First, Christian hope for the future is based on Jesus' resurrection from the dead, not on wishful thinking, guesswork, or arguments about the possibility of an afterlife. It is not just one of many ancient or modern expressions of the universal human longing for eternal life. Nor does it depend on the debatable validity of recent testimonies to glimpses of "life on the other side" by people who have been on the brink of death or already clinically dead. It is based on Christians' conviction that victory over death has actually happened in a man who died but lived again and was seen and touched by firsthand witnesses to his living presence. And it is based on Christians' conviction that this man was not just any man but the one person in whom God's plans for all humanity were made clear, so that his resurrection is the promise and guarantee of the resurrection of all people. Strictly speaking, therefore, Christian hope for the future is not based on belief in life after death as such; it is based on faith in Jesus Christ. Christian witness to this hope is witness to *him.*

Second, Christian hope for the future is based on faith in God's power over death, not on the belief that we have any capacity in ourselves to live on beyond death. As in other aspects of Christian faith, so when the question is hope for eternal life, Christians' confidence is in God, not in human beings and what they are or can achieve and accomplish by themselves. Christians look forward to eternal life for themselves and for others not because human beings are immortal but because the God who alone is immortal promises to *give* us immortality (1 Tim. 6:13–16). Christian witness is witness to hope in the power of God to make dead people live again, not witness to belief in the "immortality of the soul."

Third, implied in what we have just said is the fact that Christian hope for eternal life is hope despite the reality of death, not hope based on the denial of the reality of death. It is hope based on the resurrection of one who was "crucified, dead, and buried" and "descended into hell"—who was really, totally dead and cut off from the God of the living. Christian hope does not offer trivial and false comfort to dying people and their loved ones by assuring them that death is not so bad after all, since it is only a "passing on" or "passing over" or "passing through." Such refusal to accept the terrible finality of death, and the very real suffering, sorrow, and loss that go with it, is not really Christian nor does it really comfort and help. What is Christian and what does comfort and help is witness to a God who is stronger than death and promises to create new life and a brand-new beginning when from our side there is only the *end* of life. (There is good biblical reason to hope that this "new creation" is not postponed to the distant future but takes place immediately at the point of death: Luke 23:43.)

Fourth, Christian hope for the future is hope for the *fulfillment* of human creaturely life, not hope for *escape* from it. God raised the man Jesus from the dead. The risen Jesus was the same human person he had been before. What Christians look forward to for themselves and for others, therefore, is the resurrection of the body, not some kind of purely spiritual suprahuman form of existence. This does not mean that we hope for the resuscitation of our present bodies. But it does mean that we hope for a new and transformed life for the same personal, individual, embodied human beings we are now—a life that is still creaturely life, but creaturely life freed of all physical limitations, suffering, and death.

How do Christians bear witness to the hope for the future we have briefly outlined in these four points? By talking about it, of course (taking care to distinguish authentic Christian hope from the various distortions of it we have mentioned). But our talk will be convincing only when we demonstrate it in face of our own, our families', and our friends' suffering and dying. One of the best opportunities for such personal demonstration comes when we plan and attend Christian funerals. A funeral marks the end of creaturely life. It is a time when Christians too honestly acknowledge the grief, loneliness, fear, and even anger that all people feel when creaturely life runs out or is cut off—even when death comes quietly and peacefully at the end of a long and full life or as welcome relief from prolonged suffering or severe limitation of human potential. There is no reason why we should try to cover up these human feelings with false piety or stoic resignation. We too can acknowledge with the apostle Paul that death is the "enemy," God's enemy as well as ours (1 Cor. 15:26). But for Christians funerals also mark the beginning of a brand-new life free from everything that has restricted and tormented people in "this life." Christian funerals, then, should be not just mournful rituals but also joyful, thankful celebrations. Along with the hymns of comfort, we should sing some hymns of gladness and triumph. We ought to read and hear the great scripture passages that confess the power of God over death with exhilaration rather than with the usual "funereal" tone of voice and attitude. The prayers should be prayers of thanksgiving for the future that lies ahead as well as remembrance of life now gone and the needs of those left behind. Forced cheerfulness is no more appropriate at Christian funerals than unrelieved gloom. But funerals are a time when Christian individuals and the whole Christian community can bear witness to our hope for the future by conducting ourselves as if we really mean it when we confess, " 'Death is swallowed up in victory.' . . .

Thanks be to God, who gives us the victory through our Lord Jesus Christ" (1 Cor. 15:54, 57). How can we expect others to take seriously our witness to the liberating power of God over suffering and death if we do not behave as if we take it seriously ourselves?

When we thus demonstrate our hope for the future in the face of our own death and that of those closest to us, we have the right to bear witness to it also in the face of the death of others. We read in the newspapers and see on TV that we are surrounded by suffering and death. War, starvation, neglect or persecution of minorities, natural disaster, disease, personal violence, the ever-present threat of a nuclear holocaust—in one way or another, death and the threat of death seem to be the primary fact of life for everyone, everywhere. It is understandable that many despair of finding any meaning in the world or in their own lives. It is understandable that many protect themselves against such despair by closing their eyes and ears, becoming apathetic to the suffering and death all around them, and giving themselves to a crude or refined quest for their own pleasure and security.

But Christians are people who know that suffering and death are not the end of the story. It was not the end of the story of those six million Jews who died in Nazi concentration and extermination camps. It is not the end of the story of those hundreds of thousands of displaced people who have died and are dying in refugee camps today. Or of all those African and Asian babies with bloated bellies and vacant eyes dying in their parents' arms. Or of all those people claimed every day by cancer. Or of all those victims of the latest earthquake or hurricane. Christians know that the story of every human being continues—or, rather, starts afresh—after death. Therefore they are people who have hope for every human being: those who have already died, those who still live on the brink of death, and those who will die sooner or later in one way or another. We bear witness to this hope simply by continuing to be a stubbornly hopeful people, even when there seems to be no good reason for hope, even when everyone else gives up hope, despite everything we read in the paper or see on TV.

We emphasize once again that this hopefulness cannot become a new excuse for indifference to the suffering and death all around us. How could we bear witness to the Christian hope (and who would believe us) if we were indifferent to the suffering and dying of people to and for whom we proclaim hope? How could we bear convincing witness to hope for future liberation if we did not recognize and join in God's work in all the scientific and political human efforts to combat suffering and death in the present? But how can we expect people to take seriously our hope for the future God promises if we become overwhelmed by despair, when these efforts are not successful, and act as if death really is the end of the story? We bear witness to the liberating power of God by remaining, despite everything that seems to contradict our hope, a people who are hopeful for the future—God's future and therefore the future of every single one of God's creatures who ever has lived or will live.

The Liberating Power of God and Poor Oppressed Sinners

The God we come to know in Jesus Christ is present and at work in the world not only as the friend and companion of sinful people but also as the God who liberates them from their sinfulness. In the language of classical Christian theology, God is a gracious God whose grace is both "justifying" grace that forgives, accepts, and befriends unworthy sinners just as they are, and "sanctifying" grace that frees them from their sinfulness and enables them to become what God created and destined them to be.

We were created and are destined to be human beings whose humanity is fulfilled in loving and receiving love in relation to God and other people. Our sinfulness is our attempt in all kinds of ways to live without or against God and other people, or to use them for the sake of achieving and maintaining our own comfort, security, power, and happiness. Sin is our inability and unwillingness to love and let ourselves be loved.

In some ways our poverty and oppression in this sinfulness are even greater than that in our creatureliness. It is possible to be severely limited, handicapped, or threatened in one's creaturely existence and yet wonderfully human (more human than others who in other respects are far better off) in one's capacity to love and receive love. But to the extent that we cannot and will not love and be loved, we contradict and destroy our humanity itself. All of us need liberation from everything that threatens and destroys our creaturely existence, but even more than that we need liberation from the sinfulness that destroys our *human* existence.

Christians are people who thankfully and obediently bear witness to the God who in the crucified and risen Jesus promises liberation also in this second sense. Christian witness is witness to hope for the liberating power of God that makes people free—free from sin, free for God and fellow human beings, and therefore free to be truly human.

Hope for Genuinely Human Life in the Present

All human beings long for freedom, fundamentally freedom to fulfill their own humanity, freedom to be human. The good news of the gospel of Jesus Christ is that there is a God who promises to give us the freedom we all long for. This gospel proclaims full and complete freedom to be completely and perfectly human only as a future hope, hope for the "next life" when present human life reaches its end and goal. But it also promises that in the living and risen Christ (himself the perfect example, source, and guarantee of freedom to be human) God is at work also in this life, in this world, to set people on the road toward the perfect freedom and fulfilled humanity that is their destination.

If Christian witness to this liberating power of God is to be clear and convincing, we have a twofold task to perform. First, we must defend the Christian understanding of free human life against alternative ways of understanding it (not in order to prove that Christians and their true faith are superior to non-Christians and their false faith or lack of faith, but in order to bear witness to the liberating power of God that we Christians need as desperately as non-Christians). Second, we must offer some evidence that the true freedom and genuine humanity Christians hope for is not just an "impossible dream" but a possible hope (the true hope for non-Christians as well as for Christians). In what follows we will address ourselves briefly to these two tasks.

There are a number of alternatives to the Christian way of understanding the meaning of free human existence, but we will deal here only with one that is probably the most popular in Western society in general and above all in the United States—even among some who call themselves Christians. (It is more painful and more controversial, but it is better to confess our own sins before we confess the sins of others.) We refer to theoretical and practical individualism.[2]

Individualists are people who think that to be really free means to be free from all limitations, responsibilities, and obligations imposed on them, either by God or by other people. For them a truly free human being is one who is totally self-sufficient, self-contained, and self-centered, neither owing anything to anyone nor needing anyone for anything, able to be and do whatever he or she pleases (so long, of course, as it does not infringe on others' freedom to do the same). For individualists, responsibility to and for the welfare of others—or the suggestion that they might need to learn something from and be enriched by what others have to offer—means the restriction of their freedom, especially when "others" means people who do not belong to their own immediate circle of family and friends, people whose race, culture, economic class, national loyalty, or moral standards are different from their own. Even within the narrow circle of family and friends, commitment and faithfulness are legitimate only to the extent that they do not limit but enhance "freedom to be me."

Many who yearn for the freedom of such absolute self-sufficiency would not express it so blatantly. Many would agree that it is a good thing to care about others to the extent that one *chooses* to do so and to the extent that it does not restrict one's own self-interest. Many would even insist on the importance of believing in and serving God—to the extent that religion promotes and defends their own personal happiness and success. Many would admit that it is sometimes unfortunately necessary to ask God and other people for help. Most know that unencumbered independence is not completely achievable in a world in which we have to make allowance for competing rights and claims of others. Nevertheless, for them totally self-sufficient humanity free from all external limitations and responsibilities is the ideal.

Christians can only flatly oppose such rugged individualism (even when their opposition seems "un-American"). We oppose it not because we are against but just because we are *for* those who seek freedom to be human in such a self-defeating way. In seeking freedom from responsibility to and for God and other people, they only fall into slavery to themselves and their self-centeredness. In seeking their humanity in such lonely isolation, they only make themselves inhuman. The individualism in which they seek their salvation is really their damnation. The more successful they are in their quest for the treasure of human freedom in this direction, the more poverty-stricken their humanity will be and the more oppressed they will be by their (let us call it by name) sinfulness. For their own sake, then, Christians must oppose them and offer a quite different understanding of what really free humanity is.

True human freedom is freedom that reflects the freedom of the God who meets us in the history of Israel and in Jesus Christ. God's freedom is precisely *not* freedom to dwell in majestic self-sufficient loneliness. It is freedom to be a covenant-making and covenant-keeping God whose divine freedom is freedom to be with and for God's chosen people and, through them, with and for all people. It is God's freedom to be their faithful partner, not their self-serving and self-protecting rival. It is God's freedom not only to want but in a sense to depend on these human partners for the fulfillment of God's plans for the world.

We cannot, of course, seek a direct correspondence between God's freedom and human freedom. God's freedom is freedom to be God— over us as well as with and for us. Human freedom is freedom to be human—under God and *not* over but only with and for our fellow human beings. Nevertheless, there is a similarity between God's freedom and the freedom of human beings created in the image of God. This similarity becomes clear when we look at the humanity of Jesus and the true human freedom that characterized his life. True human freedom is Jesus' freedom not *from* but *for* other people—including people who are socially and politically unimportant or dangerous and people who are morally and religiously unworthy and undeserving. It is Jesus' freedom to accept as well as to give love—even with such people as these. True human freedom is Jesus' freedom not from but for obedience to the one great commandment that we should love God with all our heart, mind, and soul, and our neighbors as ourselves.

Real human freedom to be really human, then, is freedom *from* self-enslaving and self-defeating individualism—the sinful individualism that lurks in us all. It is freedom *not* to have to go it alone, freedom to be with others in a relationship of mutual giving and receiving, helping and being helped. Authentic humanity is humanity that is freed from the burden of the constant anxiety, suspicion, and hostility that inevitably go with the never-ending battle to guard and protect one's own independence and superiority against the demands of God and other people. It is humanity that is fulfilled in glad and willing acceptance both of the responsibilities and of the benefits of life in community.

But it is not enough to set the Christian understanding of human freedom and free humanity over against that of sinful individualism. We cannot expect people to buy the Christian view unless we can offer them some reason to believe that it is more than just a beautiful but impractical ideal. We have to offer some evidence that it is a realistic hope both for individual human life and for human society.

How can we do this? We would defeat our own purposes if we moved too quickly to point to ourselves or to the church as such evidence. The sins of self-serving and self-protecting individualism are all too obviously present in our own lives and in the life of the church. At this point too we cannot bear witness to what we Christians are and what *we* do; we can only bear witness to what *God* is and promises to do. In the present context, that means bearing witness to our hope for the liberating power of God so great that it can overcome our own as well as others' sinfulness and enable us as well as them to achieve genuinely free humanity and genuinely human freedom. How, then, can we fulfill this task?

In the first place, we can oppose sinful individualism both inside and outside the church with an attitude of fundamental friendliness, compassion, and goodwill toward those who are committed to it. Christian witness has good news to offer these sinners too, the good news of a God who wills for them the very freedom and self-fulfilling humanity they themselves so desperately seek and so tragically lose by seeking it in the wrong direction.

This does not mean that Christian witness to God's gracious will toward sinful individualists does not include a clear word about God's judgment against their sinfulness. But it does mean that even the necessary word of judgment can be spoken only with an attitude of compassionate concern for these poor sinners who are so oppressed by their sinfulness. In their personal relationships and in their political, economic, and even religious commitments they keep thinking that freedom and self-realization mean freedom from responsibility to and for others, freedom from the vulnerability and "weakness" that results from admitting their need for the help and love of others. They keep thinking that they will be free and self-fulfilled only as they "look out for number one." To this end they move from one place to another, marry or divorce or remarry, take or change jobs, read the latest self-help book, buy the latest "in" clothes or automobiles, join or change political parties and even churches—all in a futile quest for freedom and self-fulfillment just where they are not to be found. How can Christians not have compassion (share God's compassion) for such lonely, lost, self-defeating people? How can we expect them to hear and believe our witness to the liberating power of God to make them really free and really self-fulfilled—free to love and be loved—if we approach them only as enemies to be defeated, suggesting by our attitude and words that our real motive is only to prove that they are wrong and we are right? When we approach them with such hostility, why should we be surprised when they react with hostility? There is no guarantee, of course, that they will repent and accept the true freedom and true humanity promised by the gospel even when we approach them as friends who care about them and truly will only their own good. Some may obstinately stick to their self-destructive self-centeredness. But one thing is sure: It is not likely that they will repent and enter into the new life promised by the gospel unless we approach them as compassionate though confronting friends rather than as self-righteous, finger-pointing enemies. Our friendly goodwill toward them will itself be evidence of the truth of the gospel to which we bear witness and will encourage them to live by it.

Second, we can bear witness to the reality of the liberating power of God by working as Christian individuals and as Christian communities for laws and public policies that encourage and support the cooperation of individuals and groups in the interest of the common good—and by working against laws and public policies that encourage and support competition between individuals and groups who are concerned only about their own personal welfare and those of others who are their kind of people. We cannot and should not, of course, demand or expect that the Christian way of life be enforced by civil law. People think and live as Christians only as the result of free decision, not as the result of legal requirement. But we can work for laws and public policies that at least point toward and not away from the goal of the humanizing power of God that makes individuals and groups free *for* rather than *from* mutual care and responsibility for one another. In a sinful world we may expect that our efforts will always have at best partial success. But the very fact that there are people who stubbornly keep working in this direction despite setbacks and failures, even when their successes are only small and provisional steps toward the goal—that is itself evidence that our talk about the liberating power of God is not just empty talk and that our hope for it is not just utopian idealism.

Third, we can join forces with other people of goodwill—people of other faiths and people with no religious faith at all—who work for political and economic programs and policies that encourage and support concern for the common good rather than the "survival of the fittest" or "every man (!) for himself." If we are too good or too pure to join hands with such people, even though they are not Christians and in other respects may have motives and goals different from ours, we contradict our own Christian witness to a risen and living Lord who is at work in the world even apart from Christian influences and outside the church. On the other hand, we bear witness to the *reality* of the liberating power of God at work in the world, and to the realism of our hope for it, by the very fact that we gladly make alliances with the many non-Christians all around the world who also have a vision of human freedom realized in human community and are at work in surprising numbers to embody that vision in concrete public and national policies.[3]

Last but not least, we can bear witness to the power of God that liberates people from sinful self-centeredness and brings about mutual care and responsibility by demonstrating that in our own personal relationships and in our church life we Christians sincerely desire and are at least on the way toward that goal. Like all other people, we too are still sinners who are not yet genuinely free to be genuinely human. We too live by the promise of the forgiving and accepting presence of God, with and for us despite our sinfulness. But how can we expect others to take seriously our witness to the liberating power of God if they do not at least catch glimpses of it in our own familial and professional relationships and in our everyday contacts with other people? How can we Christians expect our vision of free humanity and human freedom to be even indirectly incorporated into political and economic structures if others do not see us at least struggling to incorporate it into church structures? How can we alleviate the fear of individualists that commitment to the common good would mean the loss of their individual freedom if we do not show some evidence in our individual lives and in the church that true individual freedom is realized precisely in such commitment? How can we help them get over the fear that the only alternative to rugged individualism is communist collectivism if we Christians do not demonstrate at least the possibility of an alternative to both? We do not have to be perfect examples or have all the answers in order to bear believable witness to the really free, really human life God promises in the future and is already at work to bring about in the present. But we can help others to hope for it by showing that we ourselves want to be and actually are on the way toward that goal. This "being on the way" is called "sanctification" in Christian theology. It is both the gift and the task God gives us Christians, not just for the sake of hope for our own future but for the sake of witness to the sanctifying —liberating—power of God that is promised to *all* people. That brings us to our next point.

Christian Hope for Genuinely Human Life in the Future

Christian hope for the future is hope that the same liberating power of God that sets people on the way toward genuinely free, genuinely human life will also bring them to the goal. Because it is hope based on the memory of Jesus' resurrection from the dead, it is hope that is so sure of God's liberating power that it is confident that not even death itself can prevent them from reaching that goal. Christians therefore hope for more than just "life after death." We hope for a brand-new life free of all the forms of personal and social sinfulness that separate people from God, from other people, and therefore from their own true humanity. In short, we hope for "heaven."

If we are to bear true and honest witness to this great hope, we must first be able to answer two questions: What will heaven be like? and Who is going there? A genuinely Christian answer to these questions will avoid the temptation to try to say more than we know or need to know. It will be the more authentic and convincing the less it indulges in speculation, fantasy, or wishful thinking and the more it obeys the fundamental rule for all Christian thinking and speaking about the future: What we know about God's promises for the future is based on what God has *already done* in the life, death, and resurrection of Jesus Christ and on what God is *already doing* in individual lives and in the world through the life-giving and life-renewing work of the Spirit of the risen Christ.

What will eternal life in heaven be like? We need not spend much time on this question, because we have already answered it in the preceding discussion. It will be perfect and enduring fulfillment of true humanity, the humanity given and intended for us by God's creation, the humanity realized and promised in Jesus, the humanity that even now we catch partial and fleeting glimpses of as it breaks into individual lives and into the world by the work of God's Spirit. It will be life no longer plagued by the painful and pain-inflicting choice between freedom and responsibility, the self-interest of individuals and the common good, self-fulfillment on the one hand and the demands and claims of God and other people on the other, love at the expense of justice or justice at the expense of love. It will be life in which all kinds of people will be reconciled to each other, reconciled to God, and reconciled to their own true humanity. In short, it will be perfect and enduring human life fulfilled in perfect and enduring loving and being loved. Our curiosity may lead us to want to know more about what such a life will be like. But all we need to know is that the new and true humanity promised by the liberating power of God will be far better and more glorious than anything we can imagine.

But of course everything depends on the second question raised by this great hope for the future: Who are the "people" for whom Christians have such hope? Who will in fact reach the goal? Who is promised this liberating power of God *from* the poverty and oppression of sinful humanity and *for* the riches and freedom of true reconciled humanity? Who, in other words, are going to heaven when they die?[4]

Above all at this point we must stick to the rule for all proper Christian thinking about the future. No speculation about what a just and/or loving God must, could, or should do. No guesswork based on our observation and analysis of our own or others' faith or lack of it, deserving or undeserving lives. No wishful thinking about who *we* think ought to go to heaven or hell. Our thinking must be based only on what God has done and promised to do, is doing, and will surely complete through the crucified and risen Christ and his Spirit.

Let us then hear the good news: God is "God our Savior, who desires *all* people to be saved and to come to the knowledge of the truth" (1 Tim. 2:3–4). This God "has made known to us in all wisdom and insight the mystery of his will, according to his purpose which he set forth in Christ as a plan for the fulness of time, to unite *all* things in him, things in heaven and things on earth" (Eph. 1:9–10). "For in him all the fulness of God was pleased to dwell, and through him to reconcile to himself *all* things, whether on earth or in heaven, making peace by the blood of his cross" (Col. 1:19–20). Christ is "the expiation for our sins, and not for ours only but also for the sins of the *whole world*" (1 John 2:2). "As one man's trespass led to condemnation for *all* people, so one man's act of righteousness leads to acquittal and life for *all* people" (Rom. 5:18). Jesus said, "I, when I am lifted up from the earth, will draw all people to myself" (John 12:32). "God was in Christ reconciling the *world* to himself" (2 Cor. 5:19).

Not all these passages, or others that point in the same direction, quite say that all people will in fact finally be "saved." Other passages could be cited that speak of God's terrible judgment, rejection, and condemnation in dealing with people who persist in their sinful attempt to live without or in rebellion against God, and without or in enmity toward their fellow human beings. We must reckon with the possibility that not only in this life but in the next some will persist in their self-destructive desire to be unlimited by any obligation or responsibility to God and other people, neither wanting nor feeling any need to love and be loved (except perhaps in relation to a few others exactly like themselves), using other people and perhaps God for the sake of their own self-interest, seeking only the lonely isolation of self-sufficient and self-centered false freedom and inhumanity. We must reckon, in other words, with the possibility that such people will end up in "hell," since what we have described is precisely what hell means in the New Testament. We must reckon with this possibility not because God will "send" them to hell but because they may finally get the godless and neighborless life they themselves have desired, chosen, and spent their lives striving for. For this reason we cannot be "universalists" who believe in "universal salvation." There may be some who *prefer* the devil's hell to God's heaven—especially if heaven means being reconciled and living together with others whom they despise or will have nothing to do with in this life because of their race, national loyalty, religion or lack of it, self-righteous moralism or dissolute immorality, liberal or conservative political and economic convictions.

But if we take seriously the texts we have cited that proclaim God's plan in Jesus Christ for the reconciliation of all people, we cannot take the possibility of persistence of sinfulness in any individual or group of people as seriously as we take the persistence of God's grace. The gospel teaches us to believe that the liberating power of God that raised Jesus from the dead is and will be more powerful than the rejection of God and true humanity that crucified him. It teaches us to believe that the truth, love, and transforming power of God in the risen Christ and his Spirit is and will be convincing and strong enough to melt and change even the hardest or coldest human heart. It teaches us to believe that the will of the triune God for human salvation is and will be stronger than all the human and inhuman influences and powers, desires and intentions, and actions that lead to damnation and destruction.

More specifically, the gospel teaches us to believe that even those who go to their graves with their God- and neighbor-rejecting sinfulness will not escape the grace and liberating power of God. Even if they make their bed in hell, they cannot escape God's loving presence with and for them (Psalm 139). Hell itself will not prevail against the new humanity God intends for them in Christ (Matt. 16:18). It is true that they (along with us Christians) will stand before the terrible "judgment seat" of Christ, who will call them (along with us) to account for what they have done and left undone. But the judge will be none other than the one who died and rose again to overcome the power of the sin that enslaves them, save them from their own sinfulness, reconcile them to God and their fellow humans, and enable them to be the truly free, truly human beings God created and intends them to be. Will anyone be able to meet *this* judge, see who he really is, and still obstinately say "no" to the real freedom and true humanity he represents and offers? We cannot exclude the possibility. But would we not contradict our own faith and hope in the forgiving, saving, and transforming power of God if we believed that any lost sinner could finally reject or fall beyond the reach of God's gracious goodwill and determination to save all humanity?

Perhaps we cannot be universalists, but the gospel's proclamation of the liberating intention and power of God surely allows (requires!) us to have a universal *hope* that includes even the worst and most obstinate sinners—hope for them that even their death cannot extinguish. At the very least we can gladly heed the advice of the Second Helvetic Confession composed by the (orthodox!) Swiss Reformer Heinrich Bullinger: "We are to have a good hope for all. And although God knows who are his, and here and there mention is made of the small number of elect, yet we must hope well of all, and not rashly judge any man to be a reprobate" (Chapter X).

The problem of Christian witness to this great hope for the future of all is that it seems too good to be true. Even to some Christians! But there are three contexts in which our witness to it is most likely to be clear and convincing—to non-Christians and fellow Christians alike.

1. The most obvious situation is when we face our own death and that of fellow Christians within and beyond our family circle. Even as we give honest expression to the feelings of pain, suffering, and loss that is normal and proper for Christians too when death touches us, this can be the opportunity to prove that we really mean what we confess about our hope for the liberating power of God. For Christians, death means not only coming to the end but reaching the goal of life. Christians face death confident that the God who has set us on our way and been our friend and companion as we go toward the genuinely free and human life for which we were created—that same God will also lead us to our destination. Death means that we are "free at last"—free not only from the creaturely poverty and oppression that plagues even the healthiest and longest and happiest life, but free also from the poverty and oppression of the continuing sinful self-centeredness that constantly threatens to separate even the most committed Christians from God, their fellow human beings, and their own true humanity. For Christians as for everyone else, death is indeed the sad (though sometimes welcome) end of life, but it also marks the beginning of a triumphant new life fulfilled in perfect and enduring love and being loved in relation to God and fellow human beings.[5]

Such an attitude does not, of course, prove the validity of Christian hope for a future beyond death. Some accuse us of only whistling in the dark. But Christian confidence in the face of death is a powerful witness to the sincerity of our proclaimed hope in the liberating power of God. And as a matter of fact it does happen that when some non-Christians see and hear how really faithful Christians face their own death and that of their loved ones, they are often at least interested enough to think seriously about such hope in such a God. This has been true even of some atheistic Marxists, whose hope for a world free of injustice and oppression is called radically into question by their belief that death is the tragic end for millions of oppressed people and of those who fight oppression. Especially when they learn that authentic Christian hope for the future is hope for the fulfillment of rather than for escape from genuinely free human life in community, some Marxists have been open to hear more about these strange Christians and their God.[6]

2. If Christians have a great opportunity to bear witness to the liberating power of God when they face their own death and that of fellow Christians, they may have an even greater opportunity to do so when they face the death of non-Christians. Non-Christians are people who have never had a real opportunity to set out on the Christian way toward the genuinely free humanity God intends for all, some because they have never heard the gospel, others because they have heard only distorted versions of it that should be rejected, still others because they have been unable to accept what Christians say because of the way Christians live. Other people are not Christians because they have heard the gospel but have been stubbornly or fearfully unwilling to set out on the Christian way. Some have given up and dropped out because they did not really try or tried hard but failed. What would happen if at the death of such people Christians spoke and acted in confidence that their final destination too is determined by the reconciling and transforming power of God to liberate them from the poverty and oppression of their sinfulness and unbelief? Some people (including some who call themselves Christians) would be offended by such an attitude. They want unbelievers (especially "bad" ones) to "get what they deserve," and they think of hell even if they do not say the word. But others, non-Christians and Christians alike, might hear and understand for the first time the good news that salvation really is by God's grace alone and that God is always, with everyone, perfectly just *and* perfectly loving. Some might be moved by such a demonstration of authentic Christian faith and love to become seriously committed Christians themselves. In any case, what clearer witness could we make to Christian hope for God's liberating power than by expressing in attitude, word, and action our confidence that it is powerful enough to set free to be human even those who *die* trapped or having trapped themselves in their sinful inhumanity? Our "good hope" for them is witness to our good hope in the invincible liberating power of God.

3. Witness to Christian hope for the liberating power of God comes too late, however, if it begins only when we face our own and others'

death. We cannot expect our hope for the future to be taken seriously
if we do not live in such a way that we expect and bear witness to signs
of God's liberating power breaking into everyday life here and now. One
of the best ways we can do this is to demonstrate the Christian alternative
to the hopelessness on the one hand and the false hopes on the other—
and the pendulum swing from one to the other—that are characteristic
of many people in our time (as in all times).

There is a good deal of evidence to support the hopelessness many feel
as they look at their own lives, the lives of some they care about most,
and human life in general. Personal experience seems to teach that there
are people whose humanity is so poverty-stricken and oppressed that
they simply have no capacity or potential for meaningful relationships.
They seem to be fundamentally unloving and unlovable. Or they are
inescapably trapped in self-destructive addiction, habits, or patterns of
life. Or they have proved themselves to be unchangeably irresponsible or
compulsive, uncontrollably self-despising or self-indulging, or constitu-
tionally unable to trust and commit themselves to anyone (including
God) or anything. Moreover, there seems to be scientific evidence to
support our experience that there are such people. Are we not all determined to be and remain the kind of people we are as the result of all kinds
of psychological, familial, sociological, political, and economic influences over which we have no control? No wonder that many give up on
themselves and on others as "hopeless cases" for whom nothing can be
done, for whom change is impossible, who from the beginning are
damned to the hell of their alienation from God, from other people, and
from their own true humanity. No wonder that many sink into cynical,
resigned, or despairing hopelessness and finally into deathly apathy as
they look toward the future.

But Christians bear witness to their hope in God and therefore to their
"good hope for all" by their conviction that there *are* no hopeless cases
and by refusing to give up on anyone (including themselves), despite
what personal experience or "scientific evidence" may indicate about the
lack of human potential of people caught in the consequences of their
own or others' sinful or crippled humanity. Christians are people who
believe that what is humanly impossible is nevertheless possible with
God. They bear witness to this faith by living with themselves and with
others in confidence that change, new beginning, new potential for
human wholeness, and movement toward that goal are always possible
for everyone.

This hopefulness has nothing to do with naive optimism about human
potential as such or confidence in the ability of people (even Christians)
to change and renew themselves and other people if they just work at it
long enough and hard enough. There are many things we can do to

improve and get hold of ourselves and to help others to do the same—
everything from going on a diet or taking up jogging to going into
therapy or getting involved with Christian or merely humanitarian proj-
ects. But while these efforts may help with the symptoms, they do not
get to the root of the problem, our inability and unwillingness really to
love and be loved. Confidence in human self-help schemes and strategies
only leads to disappointment and finally back to the hopelessness we
have described. Christian hopefulness for the "good of all" is not based
on hope in any of these self-liberating and self-transforming efforts,
however. It is based on hope in the liberating and transforming power
of God. Of course this power can and does work through human efforts,
including the efforts of non-Christians, to achieve human wholeness. But
Christians believe that it can and will continue to work even when the
very best and most serious efforts fail. They bear witness to the liberating
and transforming power of God by stubbornly hoping and working for
human wholeness even when there is no human capacity or potential for
it, even when people have given up on themselves and others in despair.

We must immediately add that Christian hopefulness also has nothing
to do with false and cheap imitations of it that promise that if people will
just "turn their lives over to the Lord" or "accept Christ as their Lord
and Savior" their lives will be miraculously transformed overnight, all
their problems instantaneously solved, and all their needs and desires
immediately satisfied. Encouraging such pious expectations is even worse
than encouraging hope in human potential and self-help. It leads not just
to the hopelessness that comes from lack of faith and hope in ourselves
(which could be a step toward faith and hope in God) but to the far more
serious hopelessness that comes from lack of faith and hope in the God
from whom alone real help can come. The Christian gospel does not
promise instant perfection and bliss. So far as the present life is concerned it promises "only" that through the living Christ and his Spirit
the liberating and transforming power of God that will finally create a
perfect new humanity in the future is already at work in the world here
and now to set people on the way toward that goal. It assures us "only"
that no life is so unalterably determined by one's own or others' mistakes,
failures, and sinfulness that no change, growth, or movement toward the
goal is possible. Honest Christians know from their own experience and
openly confess that no one ever arrives at the goal in this life and that
progress toward it is always slow, painful, and marked by all kinds of
detours, setbacks, and failures. They have themselves experienced and
can promise others the forgiving and helping friendship and companionship of God on the way, but they make no false promises or grandiose
claims about how wonderful, easy, and problem-free the way will be.
Hopeless people will be more likely to claim and live by the future

promise of God's liberating and transforming power if we are modest about what it means in the present. It will be enough to encourage them to give up their hopelessness about themselves and others if there is evidence in the lives of Christians themselves, and in the lives of others whom Christians refuse to abandon, that it is possible by the grace of God to make at least small changes, take at least a few steps, make at least a little progress that are signs and promises of more to come: the final great liberation from the poverty and oppression that in one way or another deprive all of us of the genuinely free and genuinely human life God intends and promises to all of us.

The Liberating Power of God and the
Politically and Economically Poor and Oppressed

The God whom we come to know in Jesus Christ is concerned about the present and future welfare of every single human being, a God who is and will be at work in the world to liberate all of us from the poverty and oppression of our creaturely neediness and sinfulness. But this God is especially concerned about the present and future welfare of those in the world who are politically and economically poor and oppressed, those who are homeless, hungry, unable to care for and defend themselves and their families, ignored or rejected as strangers and aliens, excluded or exploited because of the indifference and injustice of others who are comfortable and powerful. God is a God of suffering love who is and will continue to be the friend, companion, and fellow sufferer of such people, standing by them, with them, and for them in their suffering. But God is also a God of liberating power who is and promises to be at work in the world also to deliver them from their suffering.

Christian hope for the liberating power of God, therefore, is not only hope for deliverance from human neediness and sinfulness in general, it is also hope for deliverance from the consequences of human injustice. It is not only hope for the individual self-fulfillment that comes from personal reconciliation with God and fellow human beings, it is hope for a new human society in which competing and hostile classes, races, and nations are reconciled to God and each other. It is not only hope for the eternal salvation of individuals, it is hope for the coming of the kingdom of God, God's rule of justice and peace on earth.

In order to see that the claim we have just made is valid, and in order to see its implications for Christian witness to the liberating power of God, we must look at what scripture teaches us about the justice of God.

According to the Bible, the justice of God may include but is more than what we usually mean by justice in Western civilization. We generally think of justice as the fair and equal treatment of all people. Justice is done when everyone is equally subject to the requirements of the law and equally recipient of the protection and benefits of the law. Justice is therefore best administered by an unbiased or neutral judge who is impartial in meting out what people deserve, either the punishment they deserve for breaking the law or the rewards they deserve for obeying it. This understanding of justice is symbolized by the statue on the U.S. Supreme Court building of a blindfolded woman holding scales: She cannot see the difference between people but deals with all in the same way, giving equal weight to their conflicting claims and measuring out "balanced" justice according to their deserts.

But according to scripture God is not such a blind judge. God sees very clearly the difference between people, especially the difference between the rich and the poor, the oppressed and their oppressors: And God's justice is openly biased in favor of the latter. Moreover, it is justice that gives people not just what they *deserve* but what they *need*. God's justice is anything but neutral. It is justice that defends the cause of the poor and oppressed.

In the Old Testament, this understanding of the justice God exercises and requires is emphasized throughout the Psalms (Ps. 10:18; 72:1–4, 12–14; 82:3; 103:6; 140:12; 146:7). Psalm 72 is typical:

> Give the king thy justice, O God. . . . May he judge thy people with righteousness, and thy poor with justice! . . . May he defend the cause of the poor of the people, give deliverance to the needy, and crush the oppressor! . . . For he delivers the needy when he calls, the poor and him who has no helper. He has pity on the weak and the needy, and saves the lives of the needy. From oppression and violence he redeems their life; and precious is their blood in his sight.

Especially significant is the fact that this view of God's justice is characteristic also of Isaiah, whose hope for the coming Messiah is hope for one who will be the advocate of the poor and meek who are the victims of oppression (Isa. 11:1–4; 42:1–4; 61:1–4).

The same view of God's justice in favor of the poor and oppressed is found in the New Testament also. Especially the Gospel of Luke, sometimes called the Gospel of the Poor, emphasizes that Jesus, who is the hoped-for Messiah of the prophets, will put the mighty down from their thrones and exalt those of low degree, fill the hungry with good things, and send the rich away empty (Luke 1:52–53). In Luke 4:18–19, Jesus begins his ministry by announcing that he has come to fulfill the prophecy of Isaiah, saying that he has come to preach good news to poor people, proclaim release to captives, and liberate the oppressed. The rest of the New Testament does not emphasize the economic and political aspect of the justice of God so specifically (but see Jesus' warning in

Matt. 25:31–46 that whether we go to heaven or hell depends on how we have dealt with the hungry and thirsty, the naked, prisoners, and those who are strangers). Paul expands the meaning of the justice of God to include God's biased advocacy of those who are *morally* and *spiritually* poor and oppressed—those who are oppressed by their sinfulness in general and who are without rights before God. God's justice means that God "justifies" the ungodly (Rom. 4:5). We may assume that Paul includes among these ungodly people both poor *and* rich, oppressed *and* oppressors. But in agreement with all the other writers of the New Testament, Paul too believed that when God raised Jesus from the dead, God made him to be Lord over "all rule and authority and power and dominion" (Eph. 1:21), "that at the name of Jesus every knee should bow, in heaven and on earth and under the earth, and every tongue confess that Jesus Christ is Lord" (Phil. 2:10–11). It would be strange to think that such passages do not include the risen Christ's lordship also over the political structures and economic systems of the world.

According to the Bible, then, God's justice is justice exercised for the sake of those who are spiritually and morally poor and oppressed *and* for the sake of those who are politically and economically poor and oppressed. Christian hope for the liberating power of God in Jesus Christ, therefore, is hope for personal salvation *and* hope for social justice. Christians are people who are called to bear witness to their hope also for this "worldly" dimension of the liberating power of God.

As with other aspects of our witness to Christian hope for God's liberating power, so in this case Christians are called to bear witness both to what God is doing in the present and promises to do in the future— to the kingdom of God which has already begun, is on the way, and will surely come through the past, present, and future work of Jesus Christ.

Christian Hope for God's Justice in the Present

It obviously follows from what we have said about the justice of God that Christian witness to the liberating power of God will be a witness that individual Christians and the Christian church are called to make through social action taken either in their own name or in support of secular groups, movements, and party platforms that work for political and economic justice. But as soon as we say this, we run into a problem we have faced before: What distinguishes authentic Christian social action from that of many non-Christian and some distorted Christian efforts that also serve the cause of justice in the world? We answer with the following eight observations. The first and last are insights that follow directly from what we have just said about the justice of the God of scripture. The rest restate in light of the eschatological point of view of our present discussion some characteristics of distinctively Christian social action we have already identified in chapters 3 and 6.

First, genuinely Christian social action is distinguished by the way Christians make clear in attitude, word, and action that they are openly and unapologetically prejudiced advocates of individuals, classes, and nations that are the have-nots and outsiders of the world, especially those who suffer because of the indifference, suspicious exclusion, and overt oppression of others. Or, expressed negatively: Christians bear witness to their hope for the justice of God by refusing to support public policies that in the name of a supposedly neutral and unbiased "equality" actually give preferential treatment to those who because of their race, sex, political influence, economic power, or education have a big advantage over those who are less fortunate, less powerful, less able to care for and defend themselves.

Second, genuinely Christian social action is distinguished by the fact that it does not ask about the "worthiness" of those who are poor and oppressed. Christians bear witness to a God who defends their cause without requiring them to do anything to deserve it, the God who in fact came in Jesus Christ to save people who are *un*worthy and *un*deserving (people such as we all are). We owe food, clothing, shelter, medical care, opportunity to earn a living, and the guarantee of political freedom to the poor and oppressed simply because they are human beings created in the image of God.

Third, genuinely Christian social action is recognized by the way Christians defend the cause of the poor and oppressed of the world even when the policies and programs Christians advocate are against the economic and political self-interest of the particular race, class, or national group to which they themselves belong. Especially then does it become clear that it is God and not themselves they serve.

Fourth, genuinely Christian social action becomes identified as such when Christians refuse to give automatic and unquestioned loyalty to any conservative, liberal, or revolutionary economic system or political party, when they criticize and seek to correct the particular system or party to which they themselves feel most drawn, when they acknowledge that fellow Christians who have other party loyalties and economic views may also be true Christians. This ideological inconsistency and qualified party loyalty bears witness to the fact that for Christians all social philosophies, programs, and goals are to be accepted, only partly accepted, or rejected according to their usefulness in the service of the kingdom of God.

Fifth, to say the same thing in another way, genuinely Christian social action is recognized by the fact that in the last analysis Christians are always more interested in people than in causes, even the most noble causes. They may sacrifice the interests and success of an economic or political cause for the good of the poor and oppressed, but they can never sacrifice the welfare of the poor and oppressed for the sake of any cause —even if the cause is "peace" or "justice" or "freedom." In this way, they bear witness to the justice of God, which is exercised concretely for the welfare of human beings, not for the sake of some abstract law or principle.

Sixth, genuinely Christian social action is distinguished by the fundamental goodwill Christians bear toward the enemies of the poor and oppressed. Christians bear witness to the justice of God executed in Jesus Christ as they seek to reconcile rather than to defeat and destroy their enemies. Christians know how self-destructive of their own humanity are those who ignore or take advantage of the poor and oppressed. They know how desperately the rich and powerful also need the forgiving, accepting, and renewing grace of God that is intended for them too.

Seventh, genuinely Christian social action is distinguished by its lack of arrogance. Serious Christians are deeply committed to serve the justice of God in the world, and they are willing to take a firm stand on specific issues when it is at stake. But they are aware of their own fallibility, sinfulness, and limited understanding. They are willing to admit mistakes, to be instructed and corrected, and to change positions as they seek to discern more clearly the implications of the justice of God in specific situations. This openness to change is another sign of their commitment to serve God rather than to defend their own wisdom and righteousness.

Finally, genuinely Christian social action is shaped by Christians' knowledge that the complete and perfect victory of God's justice on earth will come as the end and goal of human history. They know that in our time and until the end there will continue to be wars and rumors of war, nation rising against nation, famines, earthquakes, and the persecution of the innocent and righteous (Matt. 24:6–14). They know that "you always have the poor with you" (Matt. 26:11). Because Christians also know about the Easter victory of God over the powers of evil, injustice, and suffering, and about the presence of a risen Lord who even now is at work even in such a godless and godforsaken world, the knowledge that complete and perfect justice is a future hope does not lead them to the conclusion that the cause of God's justice is a hopeless cause in our time. On the contrary, it frees them from the hopelessness that results from unrealistic expectations about what can be accomplished by even the best political and economic policies and actions and frees them to work confidently for the little, provisional, temporary victories over poverty and oppression that are possible here and now.

This means that Christian social action is distinguished from the naive idealism of some others who work for social justice by the fact that

Christians do not fall into the kind of perfectionism that demands and supports only perfect and final solutions to the problems of hunger, racism, homelessness, political oppression, and war. Nor will they participate in efforts to achieve justice for the poor and oppressed only when these efforts use perfectly "moral" or "Christian" means to the end.[7] Moral perfectionism may make its adherents feel superior to everyone else, but it does not help the victims of poverty and oppression, for whom even a *little* more justice could mean the difference between life and death or between bare survival and survival with at least a little human dignity. An all-or-nothing approach to political and economic problems in fact hurts more than it helps because the inevitable outcome is that nothing is done to change an unjust status quo. Christians who hope for the perfect and complete justice of the kingdom of God in the future, therefore, will show a willingness to compromise, make concessions, settle for less than the ideal in their fight for social justice. They will be willing to accept the consequent struggle of the conscience to decide continually whether they have demanded and expected too much or too little and at what point necessary "realism" about what is "possible" becomes a betrayal of Christian ends and means. But they will gladly accept the moral ambiguity of their decisions, and even the compromise of their own personal purity and innocence, in order to bear witness by their attitude, words, and actions to the perfect justice and peace of the kingdom of God that is slowly and painfully but surely on the way. Thereby they offer hope for more to come to others who long and fight for a world in which there is justice for all.

Christian Hope for a New Humanity in a New World

Millions of people dream of a world in which there is justice and therefore freedom and peace and plenty for all, especially for those who are poor and oppressed. Some have given up hope that it could ever happen and live in cynical, resigned, despairing, or apathetic hopelessness. Others continue to hope for such a world and believe that it could come "if only": If only this or that conservative, liberal, or revolutionary ideology could prevail. If only this or that government could impose its will on other governments. If only this or that nation had a bigger army and more and more deadly weapons. If only a war could be fought to end all wars. If only all nations would get rid of their weapons and agree not to wage war. If only this or that racial group or economic class could get more power. If only there were stricter law enforcement. If only this or that legal system could be changed. If only the businessmen or the women or the professors or the religious leaders or "the people" could have their way. The list is endless.

Christians are people who are sure that a new world with justice, freedom, plenty, and peace for all not only could come but will. They know that it will come only at the end and goal of history. Today we have to reckon with the possibility that it may come only as a totally new creation after we have destroyed all life on our planet or after our planet simply dies of old age. But to be a Christian is to believe that in one way or another the dream will become a reality. There *will* be a new creation, a new humanity, a new heaven, and a new earth. Nor does the fulfillment of the dream depend on any "if only." It will come because Jesus Christ will come, the risen and living crucified Lord who was and is and will be the liberating power of God at work in the world to defeat all the human and inhuman forces of evil, injustice, suffering, and death. We do not know just how or when or where this liberating Lord will come. All we know or need to know is *that* he will come, and that his coming will mean the liberation of the world from all poverty and oppression once and for all.

How do Christians bear witness to their alternative both to the hopelessness and to the false hopes of our time in such a way that hopeless people are encouraged to have hope and those with false hopes are enabled to discover where their true hope lies? We do so first of all simply by telling the story of Jesus—in such a way that we make clear that this Jesus is Lord as well as Savior, the powerful agent of God's justice as well as the self-giving agent of God's love, liberator of the politically, economically, spiritually, and morally poor and oppressed.

But our story will not be taken seriously unless we ourselves are hopeful people who live by the hopeful story we tell. We live hopefully by never being satisfied with the way things are in the world and by never giving up in our efforts to change the way things are. We have said that Christians bear witness to their hope for the final and complete victory of the justice of God by working for realistic and possible changes in political and economic policies that result in at least a little progress toward the goal. Now we add that Christians also bear witness to their hope for the final and complete victory of God's justice by never being content with the few or even the many steps that have been taken or the little or even big victories that have been won. They always want more. They counter those who say "Look how far we have come in achieving racial justice" with "Look how far we have to go." They answer those who say "Look how we have lowered the unemployment rate" with "Look how many people are still hungry, homeless, and unable to work." When others point out how the third world has benefited from the technology and capital investment of the first world, Christians point out how people in the third world have also been exploited to satisfy the first world's insatiable need for natural resources and markets for its consumer goods. If others speak of freeing oppressed people from oppressive left-wing tyrants, Christians talk about oppressive right-wing tyrants. They are never satisfied. They always want more justice for more people, and they never stop demanding and working for more. They should not be unrealistic in demanding more than is possible at any given time or place, but they never cease insisting that more is always possible. Christians are hopeful people who bear witness to their hope for the future just by their irritating and stubborn persistence in pushing and pulling to keep the world *moving* toward the new humanity they know is surely coming.

We conclude our whole discussion of Christian hope for the future with a warning and some good news.

The warning is that hopelessness is unbelief—atheism. To give up on the world or on any group or individual person in it as a hopeless case is openly or secretly to say that there is no God. Whoever speaks and acts as if nothing can be done, as if people will not and cannot change, as if there is no future except a tragic one at least for some people and perhaps for the whole world—that person says the world is not in the hands of a powerfully loving and just God but is controlled by the powers of sin, evil, injustice, and death.

We ought to understand and sympathize with people who cannot believe in God and who fall into cynical, resigned, despairing, or apathetic hopelessness because they experience in their own lives and in the world around them so much unrelieved need, helplessness, suffering, and meaningless or tragic death. Indeed, the more serious we Christians are about our faith in a loving and just God, and the more we care about our fellow human beings, the more we too are aware of the godlessness and godforsakenness of our suffering world and the more we too are tempted to give way to hopelessness. But we ought to be clear about the fact that to the extent that we do so we too become atheists—not just atheists who deny the existence of *a* God, but atheists who deny the existence of the God and Father of Jesus Christ. Hopelessness means that we do not really believe what we confess about the liberating power of God revealed and promised at Christmas, Good Friday, Easter, and Pentecost. It means not just that we "have trouble" with "some aspects" of the Christian faith but that we reject the very heart of the Christian faith. A hopeless Christian is not a Christian at all. A hopeless Christian is an atheist.

There are moments and even long periods when all of us fall into such atheistic hopelessness. God forgives us, and we can forgive ourselves and our fellow Christians when this happens. But we should not, like some, make a virtue of it by telling ourselves that our hopelessness (and therefore our dropping out of the battle against poverty and oppression) proves how deeply we are touched by the pain of others and what compassionate and tragically noble people we are. We must honestly recognize our hopelessness for what it is: the denial of Jesus Christ and refusal to serve him, the denial of the liberating power of God and refusal to bear witness to it.

But this is the good news: The hope of the world does not lie in the hopefulness of us Christians and what we can accomplish by our hopeful battle for a new world and a new humanity. The hope of the world lies in the liberating power of God and God's promise through Jesus Christ to overcome the creaturely, sinful, political, and economic poverty and oppression that sour and destroy human life in the world. The future of the world does not depend on Christians' faith and hope but on the One in whom we are invited and commanded to have faith and hope. Just when we remember and confess this, we will discover that the faith and hope we cannot give ourselves become a reality. Just as we are willing to give up the arrogant pretension—and the intolerable burden—of being the hope of the world, we can become faithful witness in attitude, word, and action to the good news that *is* the hope of the world: "Jesus is Lord! He has been Lord from the beginning. He will be Lord at the end. Even now he is Lord."[8]

We have come a long way since we discussed the strengths and weaknesses of Christian orthodoxy, liberalism, and pietism. Even when I have not mentioned them by name, the issues raised by these types of Christianity have been constantly on my mind as I have tried to formulate an understanding of what it means to be a Christian in terms of Christian witness to Jesus Christ as the presence of God's suffering love and liberating power in the world. I have tried to talk about Christian witness to this God in a way that preserves orthodoxy's commitment to biblical Christian truth, liberalism's commitment to active personal and corporate Christian discipleship, and pietism's commitment to the personal experience of God's saving grace—while at the same time avoiding the one-sidedness and distortions of each. Have I been successful? Or is the song I have sung only a new version of the theme song of orthodoxy, liberalism, or pietism—or perhaps a cacophony of all three? In the long run it does not really matter. For after all the real question is not what orthodox believers, liberals, or pietists believe and do but what *Christians* believe and do. If we have made a little progress in answering that question, it will be enough.

Notes

Chapter 1: Faith of Our Fathers

1. For an excellent analysis of the results of the breakdown of commitment to common values, goals, and paths of action in contemporary American society, see Robert N. Bellah, Richard Madsen, William M. Sullivan, Ann Swidler, and Steven M. Tipton, *Habits of the Heart: Individualism and Commitment in American Life* (Berkeley, Calif.: University of California Press, 1985).

2. A good example of the orthodox doctrine of God is found in Chapter 2 of The Westminster Confession of Faith and in question 4 of The Shorter Catechism.

3. See, for instance, *Calvin: Institutes of the Christian Religion,* ed. John T. McNeill, trans. Ford Lewis Battles, The Library of Christian Classics (Philadelphia: Westminster Press, 1960), III.2, especially sections 2, 7, and 14.

4. See *Calvin: Institutes,* IV.20, Civil Government.

5. *Calvin: Institutes,* II.2.15, 16.

Chapter 2: They'll Know We Are Christians by Our Love

1. "They'll Know We Are Christians by Our Love," words and music by Peter Scholtes, © 1966 by F.E.L. Church Publications. Used by permission. All rights reserved. Performance rights licensed through A.S.C.A.P.

2. *Calvin: Institutes* (op. cit. chapter 1, note 3), III.6–10, 19.

3. In a typical and well-known statement Calvin writes, "We are the stewards of everything God has conferred on us by which we are able to help our neighbor, and are required to render account of our stewardship. Moreover, the only right stewardship is that which is tested by the rule of love" (*Institutes,* III.7.5).

4. See Dietrich Bonhoeffer, *The Cost of Discipleship* (New York: Macmillan Co., 1959), especially chapters 1 and 2.

5. We have described here the "deist" understanding of God. Deism flourished especially in Great Britain in the eighteenth century. Many of the Founding Fathers of the American republic, most notably Benjamin Franklin, Thomas Jefferson, and George Washington, were strongly influenced by it. It has remained a strong influence on liberal American Christianity and on American civil religion in general.

Chapter 3: Rise Up, O "Men" of God!

1. "Liberal" and "liberalism" are especially slippery and confusing words in discussions of the relation between religion and politics. The same words are used to refer both to theological and to social-political positions. But sometimes the classical theological liberalism we have briefly described and are concerned to evaluate here can lead to what are commonly recognized as "conservative" political and social positions. And sometimes the faith of traditional, especially Protestant, Christianity can lead to what are commonly recognized as "liberal" social and political positions. (When Reinhold Niebuhr, for example, rejected theological liberalism and rediscovered the theology of the Protestant Reformation, he said that what we need is "a more radical political orientation and more conservative religious convictions" [*Reflections on the End of an Era,* p. ix].) When we speak of liberals and liberalism in the following pages we will try to make clear both the distinction and the relation between the theological and the social-political use of these words.

2. H. Richard Niebuhr, *Christ and Culture* (New York: Harper & Brothers, 1951); see especially chapter 6.

3. *Calvin: Institutes,* IV.20.4.

4. See André Biéler, *The Social Humanism of Calvin* (Richmond: John Knox Press, 1964).

5. For excellent studies of the political and economic thought and influence of Calvin and Calvinism, see Michael Walzer, *The Revolution of the Saints: A Study in the Origins of Radical Politics* (Cambridge, Mass.: Harvard University Press, 1965), and W. Fred Graham, *The Constructive Revolutionary: John Calvin and His Socio-Economic Impact* (Atlanta: John Knox Press, 1971).

6. The argument presented here is very carefully and persuasively developed in Reinhold Niebuhr's now classic *Moral Man and Immoral Society* (New York: Charles Scribner's Sons, 1932). This work has had a great influence not only on American theologians and churches but also on many American political leaders.

7. See, for example, José Miguez-Bonino, *Doing Theology in a Revolutionary Situation,* ed. William Lazareth (Philadelphia: Fortress Press, 1975), and Gustavo Gutiérrez, *A Theology of Liberation* (Philadelphia: Fortress Press, 1973).

8. Karl Barth emphasizes this point in *Community, State, and Church* (Garden City, N.Y.: Doubleday & Co., 1960), pp. 171–172.

9. This is the concluding statement of A Declaration of Faith, a confession of faith approved by the Presbyterian Church (U.S.A.) for use in study and worship in that church.

Chapter 4: Amazing Grace

1. In the following discussion I have learned from and developed in my own way Karl Barth's very careful criticism of Christianity understood as the reception and enjoyment of the benefits of God's saving grace. See his *Church Dogmatics* IV/3 (Edinburgh: T. & T. Clark, 1962), pp. 561–603.

2. "To each is given the manifestation of the Spirit for the common good" (1 Cor. 12:7). "Since you are eager for manifestations of the Spirit, strive to excel in building up the church" (1 Cor. 14:12). The gifts of the Spirit are given "for the equipment of the saints, for the work of ministry, for building ⌐ the body of Christ" (Eph. 4:12).

Part II: Learning to Sing a New Song

1. Although we will develop in our own way the understanding of a Christian as a witness to Christ, we follow Karl Barth in defining what it means to be a Christian in this way and gratefully acknowledge his influence on our exposition of it. See *Church Dogmatics* IV/3, pp. 554–614.

Chapter 5: Christians as Witnesses to Jesus Christ

1. Some of these witnesses were companions of Jesus who could bear firsthand witness to that "which we have heard, which we have seen with our eyes, which we have looked upon and touched with our hands" (1 John 1:1). Paul argued that he was a firsthand witness because, though he had not been a companion of Jesus, he had had a personal encounter with the risen Christ on the Damascus road (Acts 9:1–6; Gal. 1:11–17). Some bore witness to the gospel that had been passed on to them by others. It is not always easy to tell which were firsthand witnesses and which were not. But in different ways, with various concepts and images, all bore witness to the same crucified and risen Jesus. For a detailed discussion of witness in the New Testament, see the study of *martus* and related words in Gerhard Kittel (ed.), *Theological Dictionary of the New Testament* (Grand Rapids: Wm. B. Eerdmans Publishing Co., 1964), Vol. IV, pp. 474–514.

2. The words "godless" and "godforsaken" to describe our world and human life in it are used throughout Jürgen Moltmann's *The Crucified God* (New York: Harper & Row, 1974). In using these words, Moltmann has in mind Jesus' cry on the cross, "My God, my God, why hast thou forsaken me?" (Mark 15:34).

Chapter 6: Witness to the Suffering Love of God

1. For a more complete theology of the suffering love of God than we can develop here, see Moltmann's *The Crucified God* (New York: Harper & Row, 1974) and Eberhard Jüngel's *God as the Mystery of the World* (New York: Harper & Row, 1981).

2. See, for instance, Karl Barth, *Church Dogmatics* III/1, pp. 366–414.

Chapter 7: Witness to the Liberating Power of God

1. J. C. Hoekendijk: "Missions perform their service today only when they infect men with hope." Quoted in Jürgen Moltmann, *Theology of Hope* (New York: Harper & Row, 1965), p. 328.

2. In support of the claim made here that the predominant American understanding of human life is individualistic, and for a description of the various ways in which this individualism is expressed, see Robert N. Bellah et al., op. cit. chapter 1, note 1.

3. Bellah and his team also discovered in their survey of American culture that along with the predominant strain of individualism there is another strain, commitment to the "common good," which has its roots in biblical religion and in classical republican philosophy.

4. In the following discussion I intend to express my agreement with Karl Barth's doctrine of election. See *Church Dogmatics* II/2, chapter 7.

5. The last words of Dietrich Bonhoeffer, Christian martyr who was executed in a Nazi prison camp during the last days of World War II: "This is the end —for me the beginning of life." Quoted in Eberhard Bethge, *Dietrich Bonhoeffer: Theologian, Christian, Contemporary* (New York: Harper & Row, 1970), p. 830.

6. See Jan M. Lochman, *Encountering Marx: Bonds and Barriers Between Christians and Marxists* (Philadelphia: Fortress Press, 1977), pp. 128–133.

7. This is of course a debatable statement. Is it ever legitimate for a Christian to lie or steal to save the lives of hungry or enslaved people? In light of the nonviolence Jesus taught and lived by, is it ever legitimate for Christians to resort to violence in order to achieve justice and freedom for themselves or for others? Is it ever right to take life in order to save life. These are complex questions that demand more careful attention than we can give them here. The position taken is that love for God (and the justice God wills) and love for fellow human beings (especially those who are poor and oppressed) can sometimes take precedence over what normally binding divine or human law requires and forbids.

8. Conclusion of A Declaration of Faith, approved by the Presbyterian Church (U.S.A.) for use in that church.

Suggestions for Further Reading on Orthodoxy, Liberalism, and Pietism

Discussions of the history and theological content of these movements can be found in most church histories and histories of Christian thought. Following are some particular works written in easily understandable form. The work of Dillenberger and Welch is especially recommended.

John B. Cobb. *Varieties of Protestantism.* Philadelphia: Westminster Press, 1960.

John Dillenberger and Claude Welch. *Protestant Christianity.* New York: Charles Scribner's Sons, 1976.

Justo L. Gonzalez. *The Story of Christianity,* 2 vols. New York: Harper & Row, 1984.

William Hordern. *A Layman's Guide to Protestant Theology,* revised ed. New York: Macmillan Co., 1968.

Bernhard Lohse. *A Short History of Christian Doctrine: From the First Century to the Present.* Philadelphia: Fortress Press, 1978.

William C. Placher. *A History of Christian Theology.* Philadelphia: Westminster Press, 1983.

Alan Richardson, ed. *A Dictionary of Christian Theology.* Philadelphia: Westminster Press, 1969.

Alan Richardson and John Bowden, eds. *The Westminster Dictionary of Christian Theology.* Philadelphia: Westminster Press, 1983.

Paul Tillich. *A History of Christian Thought.* New York: Harper & Row, 1968.

———. *Perspectives on Nineteenth and Twentieth Century Protestant Theology.* New York: Harper & Row, 1967.

Index

Printed in the United States
1102800004B/364-369

9 780664 240134